LIVE 5

MY PERFECT THEATRE

EDITED BY: DAVID TUSHINGHAM

BLAST THEORY • MICHAEL BOGDANOV • DAVID FARR & ROSE GARNETT • PAUL GODFREY

RAMIN GRAY • LOIS KEIDAN • JOHN EDWARD McGRATH • RUTH MACKENZIE • TOM MORRIS

TIM SUPPLE • MARC VON HENNING

NICK HERN BOOKS
LONDON

LIVE 5 – MY PERFECT THEATRE first published in Great Britain as a
paperback original in 1997 by Nick Hern Books Ltd, 14 Larden Road, London W3 7ST

This collection © 1997 by David Tushingham
Copyright in individual chapters remains with the authors

Designed and typeset by 2H, 94a Lordship Lane, London SE22 8HF
Printed and bound in Great Britain

ISBN 1 85459 328 5 (*Live 5*)
ISSN 1369 0647 (*Live - all issues*)

A CIP catalogue record of this book is available from the British Library

LIVE is published every six months. Information about
subscriptions and the availability of back numbers is given on
pages 79 and 80 of this issue.

Foreword

Tim Supple
Theatre does not need theatres

Michael Bogdanov
wins the lottery

Paul Godfrey
My Ideal Theatre

Ruth Mackenzie
Jumps high!

John Edward McGrath
Idealizing Theatre

Lois Keidan
Stop pretending

Blast Theory
X Notes in no order

Tom Morris
The pirate zone

Marc von Henning
Theatre dream

David Farr & Rose Garnett
Showing the truth

Ramin Gray
reports from Teheran

Subscription details

Order form

Foreword

If you've read LIVE before you'll know that its emphasis is very much on performances which are going on now in the British Isles. This volume is rather different because it's about ideals - performances or theatre buildings projected into the future: shows, in other words, which may never actually happen.

You will therefore find a fair amount of self-indulgence and wishful thinking in the following pages. But aren't these qualities somehow more legitimate in the theatre than outside? Isn't one of theatre's functions to be a place where life's usual rules no longer apply, a home of make-believe and temporary utopia devoid of everything we wish to leave outside? So what better way of investigating that role than allowing ourselves to dream a little and seeing where it gets us? How else are we going to improve the theatre which does exist than by discussing what could make it better? The perils of going too far are slight compared with those of not going remotely far enough.

Now read on.

David Tushingham

Tim Supple
Theatre does not need theatres

Tim Supple has been artistic director of the Young Vic in London since 1993, where his productions have included *OMMA*, *The Slab Boys Trilogy*, *Grimm Tales*, *The Jungle Book* and *Blood Wedding*. He has also directed for the Royal National Theatre and the Royal Shakespeare Company.

He can be contacted via the Young Vic Theatre, 66 The Cut, London SE1 8LZ (telephone 0171 633 0133, fax 0171 928 1585)

To describe my perfect theatre is difficult.

Why? Because perfection is a frightening idea. Because one's ideals shift and to write them down, even to speak them, can make change harder. Because I fear I will be found out.

Theatre is an event, a relationship, an experience, a memory. To name it and describe its physical form can be as difficult as describing air.

The best theatre can take place in the least ideal theatres. In this crazy time of Lottery building, all of us who are building theatres without sufficient thought, experience, or resources to fill them, must never forget the home truth of truths: theatre does not need theatres. Indeed theatres can separate people from theatre. Having said that...

In my perfect theatre life is more important than style.
In my perfect theatre critics are guests at an occasion that is not about them.
In my perfect theatre we tell folk stories.
My perfect theatre is a playground.
My perfect theatre is a forum.
My perfect theatre is a church.
In my perfect theatre we do not worry too much about the influence of film, television, computers or popular music.
In my perfect theatre no one artist is more important than any other: really and truly.
In my perfect theatre we are always learning.
In my perfect theatre the performers work each day to prepare the room for the evening.
In my perfect theatre we tell classical stories.
In my perfect theatre the artists run the building alongside the administrators and technicians.
In my perfect theatre we tell contemporary stories.
In my perfect theatre the occasional empty house would not be too damaging to the state of our minds or finances.
In my perfect theatre we rehearse for a very long time.
In my perfect theatre we do not live by conventions and habits in the way we prepare, design, rehearse, programme, shedule. Each show is its own time.

Michael Bogdanov
wins the lottery

Michael Bogdanov has run theatres in Leicester, London and Hamburg. He is currently artistic director of the English Shakespeare Company, which he co-founded in 1986, as well as pursuing a wide-ranging freelance career directing theatre, opera, film and television. Recent projects include *Beowulf* for the English Shakespeare Company, *Timon of Athens* for the Shakespeare Repertory Theatre in Chicago, and *Macbeth* for both Granada Television and the Residenz Theater in Munich.

He can be contacted c/o English Shakespeare Company, 95 Palewell Park, London SW14 8JJ (telephone 0181 392 1958, fax 0181 392 1993)

My perfect theatre is a theatre in the sky.

It incorporates all sorts of performance spaces of different shapes and sizes, and is expandable and contractable. I would want bars and restaurants and crèches... and childrens' work night and day, non-stop, all the year round in all the spaces. I would want circus. I would want a drama school attached. I would want technicians' courses... In other words I would want a whole conservatoire of the performing arts so that you could provide back-up and training for the whole enterprise.

I imagine the total number of staff involved in that would probably be something like two or three thousand... (*Laughs.*)

And would it all be run by one person? The artistic director?

"No sovereignty yet he would be king on it." (*Laughs.*) No, I don't think it could be - I'm talking about my perfect space, with a whole series of attendant groups that did work outside the building, a two-way free-flow of interchange between community and the space. Because that's the way I would see it: as an extension of the community. The work that would happen out in the streets and in the schools and the clubs and the pubs and the homes etc. would be just as important as the work that went on in the space itself.

And of course the money from the Lottery would fund that and would immediately be invested - because you'd win it *twice*. You'd win the big jackpot twice - first you'd get the building and the second time you'd invest the money to provide an income from endowments.

You're winning by applying to the Arts Council for Lottery Funding or by filling out the form in your newsagents and getting six numbers?

I'm getting six numbers up *twice*. With huge jackpots. (*Laughs.*)

Consecutive rollovers.
There is a serious base to all this, the point being that the arts have to be seen as a *service* rather than a luxury. And in order for them to be seen as a service, that's what they have to provide at all levels. It isn't just a question of *a* theatre, it's a question of all kinds of different performance spaces with the right kind of training and back-up to service those spaces. And at the same time having a two-way dialogue with a community, both local and national - and international for that matter. It's what I call vertical theatre rather than horizontal - vertical because it comes from the ground, from the roots up, and cares and attends to its own community but looks beyond that local community to an international one. As opposed to a horizontal theatre which is basically planing along above the ground aimed at a middle-class national and international circuit.

And which is geared to participation on one level?
Whether its Lepage or Brook in Los Angeles, Braunschweig or Paris, basically it's the same people from the élite of the arts community as opposed to having any relation to a local community.

Your image of a perfect theatre - it's clearly rather diferent from what's currently available in this country?
Yes, well, the interesting thing is that I've been arguing for this kind of space in Cardiff. South Wales doesn't have one single major adult producing house. Or company. It has the Sherman Theatre, which is a young people's theatre seating four hundred and fifty. And there are plans afoot for a "music centre" down in the bay - they're calling it that instead of an opera house to avoid an élitist tag. Then there are other plans to extend the New Theatre, which is an old touring theatre with a very bad, cramped stage which it's difficult to do anything about.
I've been saying: Look, the thing here is to create a *new* space, maybe out of an existing building, that is *user-friendly*; where you know where the front door is for a start, that has flexible possibilities, so that you can make it bigger or smaller and you can use it for community events if you can't sustain a theatre company the year round. (Though I'm certain once one were operating such a building one could fill it with all sorts of attendant events.)
I think the opportunity to rethink our spaces is there but we seem to be moving more and more to a narrow kind of architecture that closes down the possibility of a community investing in its local arts.

Are all problems that the theatre has at the moment in our culture to do with money? Are there things that we can go some way to improving for free - or by investing other things than capital?

Art was never good for having a lot of money, it was never bad for having a lot of money, it was just different. But having money certainly does open up opportunities for people to develop. Principally - this does cost money - what's needed is a completely different attitude to the arts through education, so that you stop the divide that occurs at a very early age between those who think that if you play the violin or if you're a dancer you're a sissy.

There's a whole wedge driven very early on between children and an appreciation of the arts. It's an ongoing generational thing - if your parents aren't interested then the chances are they're not likely to want you to be interested. I think that attitude has got to be bred out via a completely different approach to the arts. We've got to breed a nation of people for whom somebody who's an artist contributes politically, socially, aesthetically and culturally to the life of a country rather than just living on the fringes of society.

Do you think that young people need work created specially for them or do they need improved access to work which is created for everyone?

I think children need to be empowered to create their own work. At the same time I think work needs to be created for them that treats them as an audience of today and not of tomorrow. In this country if you're under the age of twelve you're basically disenfranchised as far as theatre is concerned. There is so little work of value and of quality - on a large scale in particular there's nothing - and it's there that you need to look at how you work with and for children to empower them to understand and to create for themselves.

So that they don't make an enormous division between going to the theatre and watching and going to the theatre and performing?

Yes, so that the two things become complementary. Theatre is a debating platform for all the hopes, wishes, despairs, frustrations of a community at all levels. I think it should be the inalienable right of every man, woman and child to be present at and participate in events that enrich and help them understand their lives. And we're a long way from that.

I have an awful feeling that theatre is slipping out of the nation's consciousness in terms of importance at the large level. There is a massive amount of educational work going on - and the arts and drama is the fastest growing programme in schools, along with computer studies. But that doesn't appear to be impinging at the top level at all.

Maybe it's a question of what actually is the top level?

Well, yes, that is absolutely true. But I have the feeling that we're heading for an era of massive amateur theatre and very little good quality theatre at the top level.

It's a difficult thing, quality in theatre, because the proof of the pudding is in the eating.

Always.

And unless you can get round and see everything - and even then your objections are likely to be quite subjective -

And should be.

- it's going to be hard to say with any certainty what really was better than what. Is this something we should worry about?

I was going to say - no. It's not even relevant, what's better than something else. It only becomes relevant when what is praised is *not* good, and the reason that it's praised is a lack of understanding of what *is* good and a lack of appreciation of how something is put together to make it good. We're back to my spat with the critics on that really. It is a question of what is really good and what is merely show - far too often show is praised and what is good is not.

Though again reception is a complicated thing. Certain things have a meaning for some people which they don't have for others.

But then there is also this question of education - there is a blanket assumption that certain things are good because of a name attached to it or a company attached to it and that is not necessarily so. You can't just have blanket appreciation of something because you're *told* that that something is good.

On the other hand more detailed appreciation is a complex process. It's one that requires a self-education -

It requires an education, full stop. And if we were to try and revolutionise our whole way of thinking and being, not just in relation to the arts but to the community at large... If you start today it's going to take twenty years. And it's not going to start today. So that's a fairly bleak picture.

Well maybe then it becomes a different thing. One might be tempted to say: Well, some people can start.

Some people? Is it better for a few people to start rather than none at all? That's an old Tory argument.

The question is whether the people who most need to get the chance.
Yes, well you know where I stand on that. I want everybody to have that chance. I think it's *criminal* that the potential is not released in ninety per cent of our children. Whether it's mathematics or whether it's hammer throwing, whether it's dancing, sculpting or acting, the facilities should be there, the teaching should be there, the training should be there for a child to realise the limits of its capablities. And that just doesn't happen. So you have segregated and segmented groups of society where ninety-three per cent have nothing.

Paul Godfrey
My Ideal Theatre

Paul Godfrey's plays include *Once in a While The Odd Thing Happens*, *The Blue Ball* (both for the Royal National Theatre), *The Modern Husband* (Actors' Touring Company), *The Invisible Woman* (Gate Theatre, London) and *The Candidate* (Royal Exchange Theatre, Manchester). He is currently working on *Linda*, to be performed by Second Stride in 1998.

He can be contacted via The Agency (London) Ltd, 24 Pottery Lane, London W11 4LZ

My ideal theatre would not be called a theatre but a *playhouse* as these buildings were called in modern times until people began to put other kinds of shows in them, they lost their primary function as houses to present plays, and were called theatres instead. So my ideal theatre is a *playhouse*.

No-one would pay to go to my ideal *playhouse* and there'd be no tickets either because anyone could come in person during the day and give their name and reserve a seat for the evening performance with an item of clothing. The building would be situated somewhere in-between, a motorway junction, an industrial estate or an outdoor market. I'd choose a place where thousands of people pass through daily but had no particular identity before I opened my ideal *playhouse*.

There'd be half a dozen productions in repertoire and performances seven nights a week. Half the repertoire would be new plays in English and the rest would be new plays in other langauges and pre-twentieth century plays. All plays would be performed in the language they were written in.

My ideal *playhouse* would be run by an impressario/dramaturg who'd commission playwrights, select directors and choose the repertoire. Rehearsal periods would be flexible and so productions would open when they were ready for presentation in public.

There'd be no marketing, posters or leaflets and no reviews. Weekly the repertoire would be announced and broadcast alongside the weather forecast on TV and daily each night's performance would be printed on the top right hand corner of every newspaper.

On the outside of my ideal *playhouse* there'd be only three words, attached in illuminated large yellow block capitals: ALSO LIKE LIFE, because plays are also like life...

Ruth Mackenzie
Jump high!

Ruth Mackenzie is General Director of Scottish Opera. At the time of this interview she was still Executive Director of Nottingham Playhouse, a post she held from 1990 to 1997. She was previously Head of Strategic Planning for the South Bank Centre in London and has been a member of the Arts Council of England's Touring and Lottery panels, the British Council Dance and Drama panel, the ABSA national Development Forum and a board member of Dance 4 and the London International Festival of Theatre. She was awarded the OBE for services to theatre in 1995.

She can be contacted via: Scottish Opera, 39 Elmbank Crescent, Glasgow G2 4PT, Scotland (telephone 0141 248 4567, fax 0141 221 8812). E-mail: 101375.174@Compuserve.Com

For information about Nottingham Playhouse contact: Nottingham Playhouse, Wellington Circus, Nottingham NG1 5AF (telephone 0115 947 4361, fax 0115 947 5759).

Where do you start in thinking about your perfect theatre?

With artists, I suppose. My perfect theatre seeks to make what is often perceived as two different needs one need. That's the needs of the communities that the theatre is serving and the needs of artists.

That's an interesting area to look at - the idea that community and artists are distinct groups, that there's something that sets artists apart from-

I don't believe that, actually. What I believe - and admittedly this sounds frightfully soppy - is the exciting thing about art is what it does to you as an individual. Art is both transforming for an individual and it's supremely social. You know, it's the old adage, you cannot do a play, you cannot make a piece of work, without an audience. We all have art in us.

In Nottingham what we are trying to do is create the atmosphere which says that we're all on a journey. We are all on a journey of developing and understanding art and our own role in that art. We won't all end up being Peter Brook, but the aim is for us all to get as far down the road as we can. And then that process will help us to understand Peter Brook and to be active as artists - whether we end up as participants who happen to sit in the audience or participants who happen to sit on the stage. So in that sense I don't believe that there's a real distinction.

There's a distinction of quality, I suppose, a distinction in terms of the point of the journey. At some point of the journey someone wants to pay you to be an artist and at another point of the journey you seem to pay to participate. But in terms of the way in which the business of running a theatre is perceived, my ideal theatre rebels at some of that language. It rebels at the notion that says that we are there to sell things to people. No. We are all a community exploring art, though we have different roles to play in that process.

I'm coming from a theatre whose obligation, I think, is: everyone in Nottingham is paying for this place and everyone should be entitled to something, there's quarter of a million people here, they should all get something out of Nottingham Playhouse.

We're talking about a city-

Which has some very diverse communities in it. And we're trying to be inclusive with a much wider range of artists, of people at a much wider range of points on that road. We have to be everything from the ICA to the National Theatre, from The Place to LIFT, and make that look like an ideal theatre.

One of the great attractions for me of going to the theatre is always the sense of potential. This may be realised in particular ways and not in others, but the fact that it isn't realised in some ways is what makes me go back again.

That's my journey metaphor. You never actually hit a destination in the theatre, you're always going somewhere, which is good. I don't know what you would do actually if you did achieve the ideal theatre or the ideal piece of work. That's the end really, isn't it? But it's not imaginable.

So is it useful then to talk about?

Yes it is. Martin Duncan [Nottingham Playhouse's artistis director] and I and the staff wrote a thing called *SeeChange* and that is our Ideal Theatre. Every single artist and every single member of staff - everyone who comes to work in the building - gets one. For the first year we encouraged people to help us write it. Now we encourage people to tell us how to do it. One of my favourite bits in it says that one of our aims - huh - is that art should be as necessary to everyone in our community as the daily cup of coffee is to the process of waking up. And I believe that. That's a big ideal. That it should be as necessary to everybody in Nottingham. Because it is to us. Absolutely. Our shot of art is what keeps us going and what makes us grow.

How many seats have you got?

Seven hundred. But that's quite a small bit of our work, actually. We have the largest arts education programme in the country. On which we spend close on the same amount as on the main stage plays, approaching three quarters of a million pounds, on artists making shows with and for communities in schools and in community centres and in site-specific bits of Nottingham. About two hundred thousand people experience us in a year - so that's not bad if you think of the quarter of a million population. Obviously some of it is hitting more than once but not that many. On the main stage, our audiences in the Playhouse, now thirty-eight per cent of them are in full-time education. That's a lot. And fifty-something per cent of them are on concessionary tickets (obviously that includes the thirty-eight per cent). We have a really rather unusually young and poor audience - which is great.

They're going to provide an audience which will continue to be interested in years to come and then will present the theatre with a different challenge.

That journey is palpable. We started with an assumption that the rep notion of "safe" work which tends to be plays about middle-aged, middle-class people sitting on sofas and having marital problems - generalization - was not doing well. Because in our view middle-aged, middle-class people, who are the most likely people to want to watch plays about middle-aged middle-class people, are a significant minority in Nottingham. And therefore "safe" programming was not a very good bet.

Interestingly there was one moment now several years ago where Pip Broughton, our then artistic director, was having a very difficult pregnancy, and we'd torn up about three seasons and we were in real shit, actually, and we did the unforgiveable. We broke all our rules of work, namely that it should a) be led by an artist and b) come out of a partnership where you could see who in the community would respond to it. We looked at those Arts Council figures and went: Oh yeah, *The Rivals*, everyone's doing *The Rivals*, and it never does less than sixty per cent. So we asked a young director we were interested in to do *The Rivals* and he said, of course, yes - because he wanted the job, but he didn't actually have a great passion to do *The Rivals*. He set it in eighteenth-century Bath which was innovative in that I don't think we'd ever set anything where it was meant to be set. And it was a beautiful production, but nobody came, *absolutely* nobody came.

We lost more money doing *The Rivals* than we did on the weirdest Phelim McDermott/Lee Simpson experiments. And that served us right. Because you can't suddenly turn round to a community and say: No, no, I'm not on this road at all. I'm on a completely other road. The same production would have been fantastic in the Royal Exchange - it was a really high quality piece of work - but it was totally wrong *for us*.

It taught me a real lesson which is if the artist's passion isn't in it and your passion isn't in it, you haven't a hope in hell. When we were in a hole we should have said: Come on Neil Bartlett, come on Lee and Phelim, just do something. This season is fucked, we're going to go down, we're not going to make our target, we're way late on the publicity, this is completely hopeless - let's acknowledge that. Plan for failure is what we should have done, rather than go: We can do *The Rivals*, that'll pull us round - bollocks.

I think it is an important point that artists whose work has had a very great effect on you, who you very much admire, can come along and you can work with them, and for all manner of reasons it doesn't actually come off-

But a lot of it really is about whose heart is in it. In the context of reps it was very unusual when we started, and it still is relatively unusual, that we don't offer titles to directors. We expect the artists to propose what it is they want to do, which a lot of artists find incredibly difficult. With Martin Duncan we have the huge joy of grabbing some of the most interesting artists in the country - the world - who come from opera. And in opera *nobody* chooses what they want to do. So when you talk to Tom Cairns or David Pountney - David Pountney's done two plays in his life, both at Nottingham Playhouse - it is entirely foreign to him to think about what he might *like* to do. No-one's ever asked him. They say: Here's the title, here's the cast, this is the starting date for rehearsals, do you want to do it? Even if you're Peter Brook. Glyndebourne didn't say to Peter Brook: What opera do you want to do? They said: Do you want to do *Don Giovanni?*

That's also to do with the nature of the opera repertoire. There are far fewer operas to choose from.

So art-ledness introduces more difficulties because you're engaging in a debate which for various reasons artists coming from different directions have difficulty in coping with. Interestingly, the artists who have *no* difficulty in coping with this are the artists we have developed relationships with who have come from the small scale and the alternative. It is completely natural to Neil Bartlett and to Lee and Phelim that they know what they want to do.

Because they would be doing theatre even if there wasn't a Nottingham Playhouse or whatever there to commission them to do it.

Yeah, so they were the easiest people to work with at the beginning.

It's very Nottingham Playhouse-centred this. What we did at Nottingham was a very particular challenge. And for me the point of interest about it was the *ideal.* Because Nottingham Playhouse has been a stonking success we get delegations from ministries of culture from other countries, and the Arts Council send people and consultants who go: OK, how do we do this? And for me the point is not to start at the *end result* of what we do - that fabulous and exciting mêlée of art and audiences - it's to start with the process.

For us the start of the journey was to look at who *wasn't* going to the theatre and notice who they were - on the whole the young and the poor - and to begin to think about how the young and the poor might join with us to go somewhere exciting. And then to begin to think about what artists who inspired us might inspire those communities - and that ends up where we are now. Had I landed in Cheltenham or the Royal Exchange Manchester I would have stuck to that process but the art would probably have been completely different.

One of the things we thought would be inspiring, which was amazingly radical then though everybody does it now, was to start working with dance artists. That's led to a lot of very exciting dance work on the stage and in the community. Now other theatres have just copied the end result.

You get rung up by them saying: We've just put a programme of black dance in our place and nobody came. And you go: Well, yeah! Because you can't just start from the end. It won't work if you just look at the brochure and then copy it, you've got to go through a very time-consuming process of partnership.

Partnership is about making friends and you don't make friends overnight. You've got to sit around and chat a lot and have lots of very, very pointless meetings that don't go anywhere before you can get to the point where you can go: I know what you'd like. Every time you come to the bar, you want a half of Beck's. Here's a half of Beck's. But that takes a long time, before you can *reliably* say: I know what Ruth wants, she wants a half of Beck's. Actually in my case it doesn't take *that* long, but I believe that process is what making a living theatre's about.

The model you set up happened to fit not only the community but the artists that you wanted to work with as well.

Of course. That's why I wanted to work in Nottingham and not in Cheltenham. I wouldn't in fact have wanted to go and work in Cheltenham, because the journey of partnerships within the communities would have led I suspect to a programme which I wouldn't have been so obviously passionate about.

And someone going to Cheltenham now would not be able to work with the same artists because they've reached a different stage with different opportunities and have different needs-

I'm not sure I accept that because our journey has been just straightforwardly and arrogantly: We want to work with the best artists in the world. Obviously that's a subjective opinion. And: We want to *be* the best artists in the world.

And the two do go together, don't they?

Oh they do. And we started with: OK then, let's *ask* Peter Brook to come and work at Nottingham Playhouse. Why not? We hugely admire him, he's jolly high up on our list of best artists in the world. What is the worst thing that would happen?

He'd say: No.

Well the administrator would say: He'll say yes. (*Laughs.*) But one of my fundamental beliefs is if you're going to aim at the sky, then you've got to jump and you've got to jump *high*. You won't always hit the sky and sometimes you will fall absolutely flat on your face. But if you don't try then you have no chance of hitting the sky. And the thrilling thing about the journey in the last few years is that making international art ourselves has grown from inviting artists to come and share their work on the grounds that we can't make it ourselves.

Your own work never gets any worse for seeing something else that's good.

Indeed not. I think at one level having the ideal theatre means you don't have to schlepp round the world seeing the theatre you want because it's going to be in *your* theatre. That rather than having to traipse off to Paris or Berlin to see a Silviu Purcarete production or a Lev Dodin production or a Martin Duncan production, I can see it on my own stage.

When Peter Brook and his actors came to Nottingham, it sort of exemplified for me what we were trying to achieve. They did workshops with severe learning difficulties children, with other perfectly ordinary schoolchildren, with local artists, with adult education students, with university students and a sort of masterclass for local artists. They worked non-stop. We had it sponsored locally and they did the sponsor's reception. Everyone was so proud in Nottingham that Peter Brook had come for the first time, it was an amazing buzz. And Peter said to me that of all the gigs they had played in Europe, Nottingham audiences laughed in the right way in the right places. And that seemed to me to be probably the compliment that I am most proud of.

I think the choice of phrase is rather unfortunate - it sounds a bit arrogant to me to say that there is a right way to laugh and a right place to laugh.

Well, artists are. They *are* arrogant, artists. They need to be, don't they? I mean you *need* to have a strong sense of *amour propre* to think that your insight is more important than mine. And Peter is *right* to think that his insight is more important than mine. His theatre is *indisputably* a lot better than mine - you know, the work. I am not an artist. Or at least I'm not nearly as good an artist as he is. I don't mind that arrogance actually.

There is definitely something about the nature of theatre compared with other forms of performance which makes it harder for its practitioners to prove their worth, in that the sense of wonder that a musician or a dancer can achieve on stage, simply through possessing a technical skill that people in the audience know they don't have, is far more self-evident.

David Poutney says in opera the entire rhythm of the piece is set by the music. With actors, you're asking them to compose their own music. You're asking a director to motivate and enable your performing artists to create those arcs and those rhythms. And that is a very tenuous skill. It is a lot less concrete than: Unless you warm up every day your voice won't work and your legs won't work. And it is much harder than opera, music or dance actually because you haven't got the wonderful discipline or safety net that the music provides.

The other thing is that words are much more fragile. The negative way of looking at this is: Why are plays so boring? A bad night in the theatre is infinitely worse than a bad dance piece or a bad concert. Before I worked at

Nottingham, I worked at the Royal Festival Hall and I sat through some astoundingly brilliant concerts and some bloody awful ones, but you can tune out - it's not so excruciatingly, gnawing-into-your-brain awful as a bad play. And I think that's a sign of the greatness of the theatre, that it is so intrusive - so when it's good it's brilliant, but when it's not good it's bloody awful. And it's fragile because it is honestly a collective effort to make it.

Do you think we underestimate acting because it looks so effortless, and seems so natural?

There's a plus and a minus, isn't there? The plus is that it is accessible and understandable and imaginable - and words like "acting" and "drama" are colloquially used and everyone thinks that they can act and indeed everyone thinks that they can write a play. It's one of the great mysteries of working in a theatre that every single person is quite convinced that they can write a play and they all send them to you. When I worked at the Royal Festival Hall, no-one sent us symphonies. You don't get unsolicited concertos but you get unsolicited plays. I think that's very good.

I remember having a fascinating public debate with some actors complaining about their lack of professional status - why do they not have a professional status like a doctor or a dentist? But the *glory* is you know there is no such thing as an amateur dentist - there's a professional dentist and there's a not-dentist. Again we're back at that continuum, that road. Of course everyone can act and loads and loads of people do act. And there's this whole movement in my view disgustingly called "amateur theatre". Some "amateur" work is better than stuff I've paid people to do. But the glory of the theatre is everyone thinks they can do it, which is how you can then create that excitement and that partnership and that journey.

It's no doubt that the minus is that *because* everyone thinks they can do it, no-one takes it quite as seriously as they might. One of Martin's great points and one of the interesting things that we're doing in Nottingham is there is no reason why work should be disposable in the way that it tends to be. One of the ways in which you make great work is that you keep working at it. One of the reasons that we love the Maly Theatre of St. Petersburg is that they brought a piece called *Brothers and Sisters* to us that has been in the rep for thirteen years. One of our Nottingham Playhouse pieces, *The Adventures of Pinocchio*, has now been touring Europe for two years. Fantastic. Martin's just about to go and rehearse it for the fourth time. And it was jolly good when it started, but my God it's better now.

I see these things as opportunities. We can't be the Maly Theatre of St. Petersburg - it is not possible. We can't have a permanent ensemble which stays together for twelve years, but we can have a family and we can create an environment where coming to play at Nottingham Playhouse, we all get to know each other, we can begin to use those shorthands.

There's nothing really at the Playhouse that we do that's particularly new, it's just new for that sort of organization. My own background, which is in community theatre really and in experimental work, means that I could arrive at Nottingham Playhouse and introduce things which seemed radical for a regional repertory theatre but completely standard if you come from the world of small-scale live art or theatre in education or an arts centre or a European theatre. It's just somehow regional reps have got left out.

There are practical levels at which the ideals of being art-led are still difficult to deliver in Britain. The ideal is that you sit down with Luc Bondy, who we're talking to, or with Stéphane Braunschweig or Silviu Purcarete or Robert Lepage and you say: I love your work and Nottingham would love your work, what do you want to do? Whatever you want to do: that is our starting point. Well, of course actually what they want to do is generally not affordable for us. But interestingly once you are talking to Stéphane Braunschweig you find that there is no shortage of partners who are richer than you who will help you achieve what it is that you want to do. So both Stéphane and Silviu - and Martin actually - have ideas that are "too big" for the resources of Nottingham Playhouse, but we can find partners who will then help us to do it.

That's one lesson I've learned: Don't censor it out. It's back at jump up at the sky. If you come up with something that is brilliant enough, it will happen, you can make it happen. Other people will help you. You end up with these elaborate lists of co-producers in Berlin and Paris and Theatr Clwyd, all over the place... It's a very liberating process of working: just start with what you want for an artist, and then it's my job as the producer to cope with the problem.

Do you enjoy people setting you these sort of problems?

I suppose I get a buzz out of solving problems, and the more impossible-looking the problem the more exciting it is when you solve it. Neil Wallace says much the same thing. It's standard to moan about lack of money but actually it is exhilarating to raise these ludicrous amounts of money for these big projects. It is fun. It would be interesting to know what my energy would be spent on if I didn't have to spend so much time raising the money to do the things that the artists we want to work with want to do. I don't know. I could probably do my job better.

Basically the most important thing which I think we have achieved at Nottingham is a culture of love. Nobody comes to work at Nottingham for the money - the only reason that anybody comes to work at Nottingham is because we love them and that we offer a support and a positiveness - let's tell you how we *can* do this rather than let's explain how we *can't* do it. The information is identical, there's no difference, but it's ever so much more encouraging to believe in possibilities than to start from reasons to say no. And that's been the most important revolution I think that we've achieved in that building - and in that community really: that people participate with a positive attitude. I'd say that was the greatest achievement in an ideal theatre. That's the most important thing, that one is able to use words like "love" without feeling embarrassed.

Another of our aims in *SeeChange* is that the word "arty" should no longer be an insult, which is a peculiarly English thing isn't it? That the word "arty" should be an affirmative and fantastic word. One of the interesting and I think fascinating things in Nottingham is that part of the logic of your daily dose of art is as necessary as your cup of coffee is that we should be playing a very full life in the city; we should be important. And what's exciting now is that we had a big problem with arson in schools in Nottingham, and the Fire Brigade commissioned us to do an arts education project and commission an artist to write a play, to work in schools with young people to tackle the problems of arson. I think that's fantastic. The Fire Brigade have got funding problems like everybody else - it is a fantastic endorsement that the Fire Brigade think art is the way that we can all come together to try and solve a problem.

And what have the effects been?

Ah well. It was an interesting piece of work, that's the most important thing, called *Pandora*, by Mike Kenny, a new Welsh writer. It had a fantastic participative workshop programme. Now it scares me to say this - no schools have burnt down since we did that project (*laughs*). I don't think that's a reliable "output", but for me the really significant thing was I expect people like you and me to think that art is often about helping us to understand things that we find difficult, but it's fantastic that the Fire Brigade in Nottingham understand that. And we get commissioned by the Health Authority, we get commissioned by the Police, by the probation service...

The other important thing about the partnerships - which is important because there are artists who will find what I'm saying threatening - is that when everyone understands where we're going and what we're trying to achieve you don't hit problems of censorship or of difficulty. So we co-commissioned Lloyd Newson's *MSM*. In many provincial cities that would have been a confrontation point. It wasn't in Nottingham, again because the process and the communication of the process was very clear. Everybody knew by the time they bought a ticket what it was they were participating in. It was remarkable to have no complaints - I mean I've had a complaint about almost everything, the panto gets a complaint, so that was really exceptional - partly because we did work particularly hard on the sense of ownership in making this piece. Because we wanted to be sure for the British premiere that Lloyd and his dancers had a context to work in that would support them.

This notion of ownership and partnership and the Fire Brigade wanting work and the Health Authority doesn't lead to art being subservient. It leads - when we can make it work - to everybody wanting the same thing, which is extraordinary art. It's very exciting when it works. I'm making it sound sort of perfect and obviously it isn't-

What isn't perfect about it?
Well, sometimes we set off to produce extraordinary art and it isn't extraordinary. You can't get a 100% hit rate here. It's not possible. With making new work. It is a ridiculous process in a way, isn't it? Because the art only exists once it is made and is being shared with an audience. It's only then that you know whether it works or not.

When I talk to business people they find this notion of r&d through producing... If you want to make a new sort of lawn-mower, you wouldn't go straight into production, sell 50,000 and then see if it worked. You'd make one, quietly, and try it out in your back garden. But you can't do that in theatre. The only way you can do it is in effect you make 50,000 and sell them and then see if it works.

Hand them out and see how far people get.
Exactly. And obviously sometimes you get a lawnmower which just completely fails to cut any grass. All our biggest hits have been new work and all our biggest failures as well. And it's *sort of* understood - that's the hardest thing, expectations within the community are that it's going to be fabulous. People are fairly generous when it isn't fabulous, but it is disappointing.

It's important that they don't have to pay too much.
Yes, and they don't. We have very cheap tickets and that is important. But obviously if the plus is you get very active communities who care, the downside is that a work that fails disappoints us all. Nothing you can do about that really. We are now going down the road of doing more in laboratories. It can help, but there isn't any way not to fail, really. One can't be afraid of it. You have to accept it. I'm back at: If you jump up high enough, you might fall down sometimes.

To make good work you have to feel at home. And so do the community. When I was a child I sang in a professional childrens' choir, and we did lots of concerts at the South Bank. Aged eight, I knew how to get in through the Artists' Entrance, I knew where the dressing rooms were, I knew where the green room was and it felt like *mine*, the South Bank. And that meant that I had no difficulty at all then in going back to see other artists' work and going to see concerts and taking friends too, because it felt like my home.

And that's why having laboratories where community members come in, having participation and workshops and hundreds of children on the stage at regular intervals showing their talent is incredibly important - because I know that's how *I* became passionate about the arts. I felt so at home at the South Bank I had no fear of thresholds. There wasn't a sense of otherness when I went to see extraordinary artists. And that sense of open house and yet having that sense of home I think is fundamental. Home and family - family is a word that we use a lot, and it's terribly important.

Does trying to create this theatre and invest it with love, which is a kind of joint project between everyone who works there, leave you time to have a home anywhere else?

No, I live at Nottingham Playhouse, and it gets more demanding as time goes on. The more you're successful in terms of everyone feeling you are theirs, the more all-embracing it is. If I go to Sainsbury's on Sundays or if I go to the dry cleaner's or my local shop, it is very unusual for somebody not to talk to me about the Playhouse. It is not possible for me to have a day off in Nottingham - unless I lock the door of my home (my actual, literal home) and don't go out. The success of the sense of ownership means that I'm not off duty ever in Nottingham.

Given the strength and sincerity of this commitment to Nottingham Playhouse, it seems perhaps a little surprising that you're actually going to be leaving soon to run Scottish Opera. Does this say something about the limits of the culture of love we've been talking about? Why leave now?

Well, it's Martin's fault really. Because over the last couple of years he has brought a lot of opera people to Nottingham Playhouse, it's become clearer and clearer to me that opera is deeply fascinating and that I didn't know about it. Its excitement, its perfection if you want to call it that - when you've got 80 people in the orchestra pit and 100 people on stage and a fantastic creative team and this extraordinary music which brings a level of emotional intensity and communication - means it can be the most exciting theatre in the world. It really can.

So through getting to know more about the process I suppose I had an idea that my next challenge might be an opera company - but it would have to be an opera company where I could explore how artistic and audience development, how community empowerment worked. This meant really it had to be outside London - and there's three. So when they advertised Scottish Opera I felt I had to apply. I didn't expect to get it actually - it took me years to find a repertory company mad enough to take me on - but this was too good an opportunity to turn down.

I feel very untimely ripped out of the journey that is Nottingham Playhouse in many ways. One of the most irksome things is that we've set this fantastic European tour for Stéphane Braunschweig's production of *Measure for Measure,* and it's maddening not to be there. So it's come too soon, but I think probably that's always the way, isn't it? You never actually find the right time to leave. And that's the right attitude - it would be much more worrying if I'd been wanting to leave for the last two years.

Does it feel like that awful moment when the lights come back on and you have to stand up and drag yourself out of the auditorium even though you don't want to?

That's true. Though it implies that the show in Nottingham is finished, and I suppose my metaphor would be that there comes a time when the family has grown up and can manage without you. What's lovely for me is that Venu Dupha, who worked with us five years ago on this fast-track scheme when she spent a year learning how to be me - and she did fantastically well, she was then headhunted by the National Theatre where she's been ever since - and she's now coming back to *be* me. In *SeeChange* we have this important aim to grow our own stars. And we've done that both with artists and also now with Venu. I think that's fantastic.

I suppose one of the things I'm most proud of is Nottingham Playhouse *is* Nottingham Playhouse - it's not Ruth Mackenzie. Luc Bondy has been talking to us for two years about coming to do his first play with English actors - and it's Nottingham Playhouse that he wants to work at. The fact that I won't be there does not make a difference to him, which is a real tribute to all of us. So for me the metaphor of leaving is that the family has grown up and now it doesn't need the same sort of mum as it did when it was littler. So now I go off and have another family. Gosh, that makes it sound like hard work. And it will be. It's the same adventure, the same process that I now start in Scotland.

Perfection is never static - there's never a fixed moment when you can go: that's perfect. Perfection is always a journey.

Is there also a sense that you only ever discover that you actually got there afterwards? Running a theatre one spends so much time projecting one's desires into the future-

That's a very good question. We've just had our draft five-year appraisal. There's something in there that is so moving and we didn't know about it. It made us all cry, actually - and apparently it made the appraisal team cry as well! There's a special school in Nottingham for children with very severe learning difficulties which has a fantastic headmaster and a brilliant arts policy. They come to everything at Nottingham Playhouse - even the most difficult, challenging pieces of theatre - and have done throughout my time there. We do lots of work with them, and it is an extraordinary school, led by this extraordinary man. And he gave evidence to the appraisal team. And he talked a lot about the benefit of the arts for these young people and so on. But he also said that all the pupils in the school know that if they get lost in town they need to find their way to the Playhouse. Because then they'll be safe and once they've found the Playhouse, somebody will help them because they're *home*. That's a school rule - and it's so moving because that's absolutely our aim, and I didn't know we'd achieved that.

And I suppose it is in retrospect clear to me now that the Playhouse doesn't need me - that it can now carry on on its own. Venu will bring in the next generation of innovation and the next generation of partnership and involvement, and that is thrilling for me. And that's only clear *afterwards*. Because obviously part of your love for a place is that it would be heartbreaking to leave and for it to suffer - but I don't have any fears that that will happen to the Playhouse: it will fly.

John Edward McGrath
Idealizing Theatre

John Edward McGrath is artistic director of Theatre Venture in East London. Previously he was associate director of Mabou Mines, the New York-based experimental theatre company. At Theatre Venture he works with a variety of local communities and is currently developing *Across The Earth*, a site-specific production based on experiences of exile. His articles have been published in the *Drama Review, Women and Performance* and the *Guardian*.

He can be contacted at: Theatre Venture, The Resources Centre, Leywich Street, London E15 3DD (telephone 0181 519 6678, fax 0181 519 8769). E-mail: tventure@ecna.org or jem7993@is2.nyu.edu

I'm sitting next to you, my arm around your back, my fingers bouncing to the pulse of your wrist's blood.

You laugh and suddenly we separate — opposite ends of a cavernous space. A shout — the words float toward your ears with half-lost meaning. Between us muscular bodies bounce on a vast trampoline, and in the far corner a tattooed woman sings an old French song.

In my ideal theatre there are cushions, towers, pools and tiny rooms, but no chairs. Well maybe a comfortable armchair or two, but nothing in rows. In my ideal theatre it is possible to whisper in your ear and stroke your skin. Watching you become aware not only of an over-there-ness but of a closeness, an intimate potential in each word and image.

In my all-too-real theatre, I use a lot of microphones, not because I lack respect for vocal training, but because microphones provide an opportunity to explore different, contradictory, qualities of voice. The opportunity, say, to amplify the intimate mutter or sigh, to discover its potential hugeness.

In the time-honoured debate about "what makes theatre theatre", I vote with the audience party. It is these live bodies together which for me form the condition of theatre. These bodies and a prepared, structured experience.

Rows of seats make me sad. Sightlines depress me. I have built walls to divide the audience into visual camps. I have encouraged them to make popcorn or watch TV while the play is going on. I have given them Walkmans with secret messages and private tunes to listen to when the going gets tough.

Does an ideal theatre live in an ideal world? Was I the fag-end of an extended generation that saw theatre as a political choice? Do these dreams linger or did they decay into the awful thought that theatre is good for you? In my daily theatricals, I often work with people who have not been listened to. Who have something to say. To whom? These days I feel comfortable with the thought that speaking to yourself, learning the feel of your voice, is one way ahead. Shape those mutterings, add layers, contradictions, shameful desires. The quality, the danger, of the performance itself can exceed any message. What's art if not that?

In my ideal theatre the building itself is a memory. Recalled each time for its useful qualities, its structurings.

The troupe has moved on, but the audience remain — eagerly awaiting. We will need to produce something from the resources available. A borrowed ctor. A live video link. A story faxed from another hemisphere. A local uilder who plays the saxophone. Histories buried underneath the local ipermarket or carried here across seas and generations.

Despite the eagerly awaiting audience, in my ideal theatre we take time to rehearse — a lot of time. Layers are added, complexifying and contradicting. Design, music, have their own logic, they serve no-one's purpose. The audience visits as we go about our stuff and one or two become part of it all, adding layers. One evening, in retrospect, we realise that everyone was there inight, playing their roles, prepared or observational, and we know that we have opened the show .

Lois Keidan
Stop Pretending

Lois Keidan has been director of Live Arts for the ICA, Britain's flagship venue for experimentation across all artform areas, since 1992. She began working in the independent music scene, managing bands and running a small record label before moving into theatre, where she worked for Theatre Workshop in Edinburgh and the Midland Group in Nottingham before joining the ICA.

For further information contact:
Institute of Contemporary Arts, The Mall, London SW1Y 5AH (telephone 0171 930 0493, fax 0171 873 0051).
E-mail: info@ica.org.uk

My idea of a perfect theatre covers so many things.

Location is important to me and the ambience of the space, whether it's comfortable, whether you can see properly and whether you feel safe - safe in so many ways - that you understand the language and conventions of that theatre and that technically things are so smooth you don't notice them. But the most important thing is that I'm experiencing something that I could not be experiencing in any other place and any other time, that it's very much of that moment and it's in some way changing *me* emotionally or intellectually, opening my mind to certain things that I haven't realised before, or just wowing me with a dynamic or intimate experience.

I expect from theatre things that I can't get in any other media. And I think that's becoming increasingly difficult. I think that's where live art and new performance comes into its own. You're not watching narrative theatre or kitchen sink drama. The whole notion of artifice is one I just can't take any more. We're in times where we're beyond artifice. People pretending to be other people in a pretend living room and stuff leaves me cold. It's the kind of experience I could much happier get from films or television. What happens on stage shouldn't be an attempt to replicate real life in that kind of sense.

You mean replicate real life to the extent that it denies the life that's there, that the performers bring with them in terms of their lives off stage and that the audience bring with them from outside the door?

Yes. This pretence, this make-believe that we are in somebody's living room when we're obviously not in somebody's living room - and people pretending to be other people, actually. For me theatre gets interesting when it begins to deconstruct that process. For example The Wooster Group always acknowledges the artifice, it acknowledges people pretending to be people and plays around with those kind of devices.

Can you remember when you first made that discovery?

It's been a fairly longish process, probably about ten, twelve years and now - which is a terrible thing to be saying - there's very, very little *theatre* that excites me any more. And that's particularly happened in the last five years or so.

And you don't think of the work that you're involved with as theatre at all?
Yes I do. I think definitions are increasingly problematic but also increasingly exciting. The inability to define the newness keeps it alive. So companies like Forced Entertainment, like desperate optimists - they define themselves as "theatre". What I meant earlier when I said "theatre" was more conventional notions of narrative theatre, where the starting point is the play, rather than where the starting point is the idea. I'm talking about plays. And now so much of the theatre I was brought up on I really can't watch any more.

In addition to my ideal theatre space being a safe space - a comfortable space, a well-equipped space, a space you can see in, you're not cold and you're not too hot and all of those things - I also very much enjoy going to performances and events *outside* theatre spaces with all those sort of things completely thrown to the wind, and you are put in situations of extreme either physical or emotional danger. I know a superb company in Israel who present a site-specific piece on the legacy of the holocaust-

This is the Akko Theatre-
Akko Theatre, *Arbeit Macht Frei*. And I would say ninety per cent of the audiences for that have never been to anything like that in their lives. If they go to the theatre it's to see kind of West End productions of *Hedda Gabler* in Tel Aviv or in Jerusalem, but friends tell them they should go and see this event, they know nothing about it, and they go and see it. And you're really put through the mill. It's not participatory in the sense of picking people from the audience and humiliating them on stage, but a lot of the dynamic of the piece goes back to the audience's involvement, their direct involvement there, their answering of questions. And the responsibility for how to read the piece is put back onto the audience.

The most interesting performance at the moment - particularly coming out of the States - is leaving the responsibility for how they read what is presented to them to the audience. It's not spelling out what their response should be. It's not going through the motions for them. It's not cathartic in that kind of sense.
Guillermo Gomez-Peña is a superb practioner of that, where the audience have to deal with it themselves and how they deal with it again kind of forms and shapes the piece. The Hittite Empire are another example, where the whole thing is just incredibly uncomfortable. You think it's choatic and out of control, but it's totally controlled - controlled chaos. But it's what happens to you emotionally in that unstable period that feeds the piece, informs the piece and shapes your response to it.

Does this mean that the ideal theatre from your perspective is not something where you're necessarily worried about an audience turning up in large numbers?

Yes, quality, not quantity. Obviously a lot of my energies at the ICA go into trying to develop *new* audiences: a whole new generation that would rather die than go to the West End, but there's still something missing in their lives that performance can fill a lot of. For the work we have presented here we have seen a very diverse audience: people that are hungry for innovation, risk, change and intellectual and emotional stimulation. And also hungry for a live experience. There are certain companies that we've presented in our theatre where the ritualistic process of the whole thing has been the closest equivalent, I feel, to what going to church must be like if you're a believer. It is a gathering. It's a shared experience.

I am very concerned about audiences going to see work for the right reasons - which are their own reasons, but I am concerned about how work is represented and the choices that people make when they choose to come and see it. The famous stories of subscription buyers standing in the foyer saying: What is it we are seeing tonight? That to me is just total anathema. They should really want to see this either because they're curious, because they've heard about it, because they're interested in those kind of ideas, stuff like that. And the only way they *can* do that is if the work's represented effectively, starting here and then moving on through the press.

That's why we curate work in seasons. Somebody might be quite interested - or vaguely interested - in an artist's work but not really know if it's for them. So what we try and do is create contexts to encourage people to consider different ways of approaching performance. I think a lot of it comes down to the language we use, the imagery and representation. We try to be as honest to the work as possible and at the same time as honest to the audiences as possible about *why* we're putting it on, why we think it's significant, how it relates to this bunch of issues and why we feel audiences will benefit from that experience. We also hope in that process that audiences will read it and think it's not for me and decide not to come rather than come and complain about it.

Are there people who you would love to see shows who somehow you can't get to come to the ICA?

Audiences?

Yeah.

For sure.

Just thinking about how theatres operate and how they might operate in a different world because there are all sorts of contraints on institutions like this one. Institutions have to behave themselves.

People have perceptions of the ICA, and a lot of what everyone who works at the ICA's mission in life is is to break those perceptions so that the ICA is just a means of getting to see the work.

And yes there are audiences who I would love to be coming to see the work. And yet within that there's incredible degrees of complexity, which is why Catherine Ugwu, my colleague, and I have the programming, commissioning and curatorial policy we have. One of our main priorities is to really resource and shape and support the profile of the new generation of contemporary black British artists.

To me the most energetic work at the moment and the most inspirational work is coming from the margins. It's work that has been disenfranchised by the dominant culture and dominant narratives. Performance/live art has been able to offer artists new languages to articulate things that it wasn't possible to articulate through other forms, so it's proved to be a very persuasive platform for artists who have something to say about themselves, about their own issues of identity. For black artists it's been a particularly potent medium, and there is a new generation of black artists making very strong work.

That work wasn't really being resourced and supported. But we also knew that one of the best ways we could see to support that work and support the development of black audiences for contemporary practice was not *just* to put on shows. I mean, why on earth *would* black audiences suddenly start coming to the ICA just because we happen to put on a black artist over two nights? So we had to really demonstrate that there was a commitment to presenting that work and to having dialogues with audiences and artists. That was a very long, slow process for us - two or three years work of serious audience and artist development, which was to do with comissioning work, contextualizing the representation of the work, having very informed dialogues. We had a talks series called *Talking Loud Saying Something* focusing on particular issues with reference to black culture. And then also we ultimately published a book, which Catherine edited, called *Let's Get It On, The Politics of Black Performance.* There were so many people with so many excuses for *not* knowing about work they should know about, we thought if we just get it down on paper then there's no excuse any more.

And the result of that process is that black audiences for the most part do feel comfortable and happy coming to the ICA and that the black artists we work with feel very comfortable and happy working here. They don't feel that they've just been brought in for a particular agenda and then been packed off again - there is an ongoing support and ongoing commitment to their work. And we've spent the last couple of years doing a similar process with a new generation of Chinese artists and a new generation of Chinese audiences. Again to try and reflect the fact that our interest and our commitment to this really exciting work is not putting on a couple of great shows and then walking away from it.

So those are some of the areas of audience development. Of course I wish particularly for companies like Forced Entertainment, who do fabulously well when they come here, that the broader theatre community would pay them more attention. *Textuality* was a great example: I felt that the broader theatre constituency didn't engage with that series at all, which was very disappointing because that was very much our gesture back to them. I think it's because they read ICA first and what the season was second. And that always happens. Robert Lepage first presented his work in Britain at the ICA and it's not until he gets to the National that people start screaming about it. It seems location comes first in terms of critical perspectives.

Do you think it might help if there was only one theatre in London but somehow they did twenty shows a night. A huge muliplex-
Experimental turn left, traditional straight ahead - I don't think it would help at all.

We can only do the programming we do at the ICA because we're incredibly privileged. We're in London and we're an institution that is mandated to take risks. If that wasn't the reason we're funded, I would have been thrown out years ago I can assure you.

We are in a position of extreme privilege - I don't mean money - because we can really prioritize the work that we put on, knowing damn well that there are a thousand theatres in London catering for other stuff. Colleagues who run the Green Room in Manchester and the CCA in Glasgow are under a different kind of pressure because they've got much broader communities that they need to address. They are the only experimental space in town, whereas I know if we can't provide a context for a certain type of work I can, say, phone Tom Morris at BAC, phone John Ashford at The Place. It seems to have happened organically rather than by any kind of design, but most of the spaces in London I think are incredibly complementary at the moment. We all kind of know what each other's doing so we're able to cross-refer quite happily and also know that we're taking care of certain areas of cultural need. And that's a great position to be in.

I'm thinking of people who don't know where to find these things, of people who maybe don't go to the theatre at all. I quite like the idea of hijacking a West End theatre for a night and instead of getting Ray Cooney they see Forced Entertainment or The Hittite Empire-
Absolutely.

But just to go back to the one space where everything happens - I wouldn't want that, but I would want what happens at the ICA, where there are four different programming departments but we're all dealing with ideas and how those ideas are manifested in our own areas. There's so much crossover that I don't want theatre and performance to be excluded. I want it to be something to be seen to have very clear relationships with other artistic practices, ideas that are being pursued in other forms and in other ways seeing where those connect.

There are very thin walls between art forms. Film clubs are thriving because they're live experiences for watching films and there are so many art clubs. There's just a massive amount of crossover into fashion, pop music, all those things. And that's one of the things that are characterising the ICA, that we're able to have those dialogues across forms, to work together in certain ways so the cinema show, videos that document work by particular artists and we do stuff in the theatre by performance artists working on video.

Are you aware simply because you've got a finite space and finite time - without even talking about financial resources - that you can't get as many artists into the building as you would like to?

Yeah. Sometimes it's been the other extreme when we intensely overprogramme and keep getting our knuckles rapped because we've stretched the building to its limits. So the policy for this year is to programme less.

Because we have a very clear policy, we can prioritize what we do present - I think it's a very important thing for people who are running venues, promoters, people like me - I'm on a salary and most of the people I work with aren't on a salary. That salary doesn't mean that I'm better than any of them or anything like that. It means that I've got a whole bunch of responsibilities. And we're a public institution and therefore we've got even more responsibilities - which is why we need a very clear artistic policy so that when we do make choices we're very clear about why we're making those choices. We'll articulate that to anybody. And anybody who sends us a proposal: if it's got our name on it they will get a letter.

Yeah, it is tough and fortunately in the last five years I can safely say we've managed to present most of our favourite artists in the whole world. And the list of people we want to work with and haven't yet is shrinking, which is great. But inevitably there is work that falls off the map that we're not able to do for reasons of context, resources, budgets, timeframes, anything else.

Do you think a perfect theatre might be permitted or might even need to fail at times? Is a theatre that only ever has hits somehow not trying quite hard enough?

Unless people are given the space to form their language, to form their ideas, and to try that out with audiences then the whole thing will atrophy and die, it'll just become frozen. The only way it can move forward is people taking risks and trying out ideas and inevitably that's got the failure equation attached to it. But the right to fail is an increasingly difficult space to protect. And especially so in London right now where there is so much choice. If you're choosing to see one thing and it doesn't work then you're well pissed off - because you could have gone to see a film where there's no notion of that right to fail because it wouldn't be on in that West End cinema unless it had got through a whole bunch of different tests. And I think it is very difficult. Everything's so tight because of financial pressures at the moment.

Certainly when we commission a piece of work, then it is about the process of creation, it's not about coming back with the finished product. Hopefully they *will* come back with the finished product, but if the artist has been through the process then that's fine - that's the right to fail, absolutely. If they've had a fantastic idea, they've tried to make it happen, we've supported them in that process and it hasn't got there, then that's something that I really respect.

So many great things have come out of people's failings and people's mistakes.

Again it puts an onus on someone in your position to encourage the audience to have some sense of the field of play-

Absolutely and that I think comes back to how we contextualize the work and how we frame it. What we say in our publicity copy is another aspect of this. Also we firmly believe in programme notes - all our programmes are full of copious notes.

The great thing about the area where we work in is it's so difficult to describe it - and the point at which you're writing publicity copy the piece probably isn't even ready. That makes representation of this area of work very tricky. We try to get around that by trying to deal with what the piece is about, the type of forms it's drawing upon, where the artist's kind of coming from rather than a literal description of the piece of work. But you can never prepare people completely. And I would never want to - because it's the element of surprise and not knowing what you're going to get that keeps things exciting, keeps audiences on their toes.

I always find the more time I spend trying to think what might a show be like the further it ends up being from what I've imagined.

I don't think anybody can imagine what one single artist is imagining so nobody can project in that sense what they're going to see, which is another reason why I think the area of work that we represent here is very exciting. Not only will the content be consistently different and provocative but the form will be consistently different and provocative as well, which you possibly don't get at the Court, at the National, where you're dealing pretty much with a set of givens. In the kind of work that we represent here I don't think there are any givens, I think almost anything's possible.

Which is why you have to make decisions on the basis of a set of criteria which you discuss and argue about.

Yes it is. In the programming we run here we try to make it both proactive and reactive. We try to react to the work that artists are making and the ideas that artists are dealing with and create the most appropriate context for that, whether they're one-off events or whole new strands and series. And then the proactive way is we try and find a way of shaping those developments and making sense of them. So they don't become isolated kind of freakish outcrops but they're seen in relation to whole traditions.

Ron Athey is a classic example of that. People see Ron Athey's work and hold their hands up in horror and say that's a freak from the late twentieth century. Well actually he might be a freak, but he's a freak from Ancient Greece onwards. There's a whole history of artists who deal with pain and blood. Also he's dealing with Middle Ages images of martyrdom and suffering, so there's a massive continuum in his work. So to present that beside Marina Abramovic, a world famous artist who's been dealing with endurance and pain and blood since the sixties, is an example of the way that we try and be proactive. We see our responsibilty as to try and shape things to make sense of artists' work and also - as I keep saying - to make sense for audiences of how to approach it and how to react to it and where it's coming from, how it fits with other things.

There are many reasons why we curate seasons. One - something like Ron Athey - is to create a safe space for his work. And another is to problematize issues. So a lot of the very early work we were doing with black artists was to problematize issues around identity and individual experience and hybridity. Because there was still a ridiculous quota system, there was still a notion that all black experiences were the same - which is obviously a complete load of nonsense. So a lot of the work we did around issues of cultural diversity was to show that they couldn't be reduced to a single experience, and no black artist should be expected to carry the weight of some idealized notion of a black experience or a black community.

Just as no white artist would ever be expected to produce a quintessential white view on something.

Yet for some reason it happens with black artists. And also the other thing that happens with black artists, which is why it was important for us to provide resources and contexts and debate and discourse, was that so many artists still do just get project funding. This is where another huge right-to-fail issue comes in. So many artists who do get project funding get *inadequate* project funding - this applies across the board, but it's particularly true of many, many black artists - they don't have sufficient training and experience to be able to do certain things, but training and experience is not made available, infrastructure is not put in place. It's hit and run funding that's just setting up people to fail.

That's a good subject to explore because obviously part of the opportunity of talking about these things is what are the problems that you have, what are the areas in which the theatre in general - not just the one that we happen to be sitting in at the moment - what is it not doing that it ought to be doing? what do you want it to do that it's not delivering?
Most things boil down to money, but not everything. The biggest subsidizers of culture in Britain at the moment are artists and the biggest subsidizers of the ICA are artists, easily. Many of them take a huge dive in fees to perform here. The difference between what artists across the board get paid here and what they should be paid outweighs our annual Arts Council grant.

Money would make an awful lot of difference, just in terms of buying time, buying resources, buying experience, buying training, buying skills. Being able to promote, market and represent the work properly and being able to offer sufficient training and workshopping opportunities for artists.

But there's also a whole bunch of things that money can't buy which seem to be pretty critical as well, which is commitment to the work. Commitment to the work that's made evident in terms of that you're not just doing it for the sake of doing it, you're not just doing it because you're being paid to do it, you're doing it because you love it. And that kind of passion should come through in some type of way.

The other thing for me is that artists should be encouraged to be so much more involved in how things are done and have a clear say in how the work is developed, how it's presented, how it's represented, all those things. Artists are still very much locked out of that equation - I think. Artists aren't able to change things in the way that artists should be able to change things and aren't encouraged to be involved in things that they should really be involved in - and that's a constant frustration.

There's a whole bunch of people who are in the process of trying to set up a network for new work - the idea is there's national groupings and gatherings that can either lobby, advocate work, share information, share resources - but in the very early discussions of that there were promoters who felt that artists should not be involved. We're *way* beyond the days when artists should not be involved in high level decision-making about their practices.

Promoters and producers should know when it's the artists who should be setting the agenda. *But* promoters and producers *do* have a critical role to play. A recent Arts Council Fund in Combined Arts is for artist-led initiatives. That's the main fund for live art and combined arts projects. And that again just seems to be inviting artists to fail because artists shouldn't be expected to do what we (i.e. promoters) do.

And even if they can do it, not to be expected to do it at the same time.

It's a very symbiotic relationship, the artist-promoter one, and I think they should both be accountable to each other in a completely equitable relationship. And obviously it's *not* because I'm the person saying yes or no. And it's not because I'm the person on salary.

I think I can give you a definition of my perfect theatre now.

My perfect theatre is where there's no expectations of form or where there's no artistic orthodoxy in that kind of sense, that's going to take me places emotionally, intellectually where I haven't been before, that's going to make me think, that's going to move me in some sort of way, that's going to raise either implicitly or explicitly very key issues about life, death - issues that relate to the world in which we live - and that speaks of our times in the language of our times. That's it.

That's very succinct. How have you arrived there?

Probably by just looking at the work that's had the most impact and influence on me, that's stayed with me and that's been influential on other work that I've appreciated. I grew up in Liverpool, and I was dragged off to see the RSC, which I hated enormously until I was about fourteen. Then I was taken to the Liverpool Everyman, which was an incredibly dynamic, vibrant lively space that was right at the heart of the city's soul, where you'd always have a stimulating, exciting, entertaining experience, where the work was trying to deal with something. There was lots of sickness, lots of bad taste, lots of shock, lots of humour - very disquieting, stimulating, provocative experiences and you didn't know what would happen next. And it was work that was accessible to everyone in Liverpool. It wasn't élitist in that sense - it talked in the language of its time.

What shows would those have been?

Oh God. There was a fantastic production of *Sweeney Todd* where they served meat pies in the interval. I can't remember the names of any of the Christmas shows or the other stuff, but it was a very different experience from going to say the Liverpool Playhouse down the road, which was touring rep theatre that I just found boring: "Get me home, get the television on, get the record player on." The Everyman seemed to offer things that the television and the record player gave, which was stimulating and contemporary: radical sparkle.

Blast Theory
X Notes in no order

Matt Adams and Ju Row Farr are two of the founder members
of Blast Theory, a group of five artists who make live events,
installations and films. In 1998 you will have the chance to be
kidnapped by Blast Theory for forty-eight hours.
Call 0800 174 336 for details.

Matt and Ju are currently on a one-year residency at the
Kunstlerhaus Bethanien in Berlin.
For further information contact:
Blast Theory, Toynbee Studios,
28 Commercial Street, London E1 6LS
(telephone/fax 0171 375 0885).

E-mail: blasttheory@easynet.co.uk

X Paul Virilio makes the point that the history of the last two centuries is a transition from the importance of territory to the importance of time. In World War One (running time: 1566 days)a gain of 100 yards was a victory; in the Gulf War (running time: 44 days)the timing and speed of the attack was the critical factor. In movies like "Speed" and "Twister" everything is travelling fast throughout giving the audience an adrenal rush, a sense of giddiness, a visceral experience: theatre must respond to this by becoming more layered, more surprising and just plain quicker.

X Notes in no order

IV A perfect theatre is one that can create an event, that celebrates its live purpose. It has room for uncertainty and contradictions. It is distinct from other theatres, it is a space in constant use.

IX A perfect theatre doesn't have black walls.

III The most perfect piece of design evident in modern theatres is the lighting system: a grid which allows a light to be placed anywhere and an almost infinite array of different lights to put on it. In a perfect theatre every element – seating, staging, walls, floors, entrances and exits – would be like this: fluid, mobile, open to unlimited permutations.

IIX To the traditional technical extras of gobos and colour wheels must be added video projections and new technologies. On top of stage fighting skills and provincial accents we must add everything from dance and BMX skills to using a video camera and kick boxing.

VII Perfect theatre has multiple viewpoints, physically and mentally. It allows an audience to choose different places from which they can watch and allows them to interpret what they see according to their own perspectives.

I More travelling space: like cinema, like cars and trains, like dreams theatre should be able to allow motion, a sense of travelling. Traditional foyers are like airlocks full of people waiting; waiting for drinks, for tickets, for coats, for programmes, for the bell to ring. Auditoria shouldn't have crammed seats and aisles that insist that you either knock into the knees of those already seated or sit waiting to have your knees knocked by someone else. Once the performance has begun there should still be a sense of motion: taut, passionate writing, motorised staging, film, video and energetic performers will immerse the audience in a different world. Mega-musicals and theme parks have much to teach us.

V When theatres have video games, cinemas, bars, DJs, Internet connections, TVs, chill out rooms, video libraries then they will start to approach perfection. They will have understood what commerce and entertainment have to offer, that challenges, shocks, energy and passion can come from unexpected sources.

VI A perfect theatre has internally wired lighting bars on motorised winches, golden scans, decent showers, motorised retractable seating, a massive sound system, dozens of 13amp sockets and an audience beating on the doors.

II FLUID - performances happen in foyers, toilets and corridors. Audiences watch from balconies, basements and the bar. They can control their proximity to the action, how long they watch and at what time of day.

Tom Morris
The pirate zone

Tom Morris worked as a journalist for the *Sunday Times*, the *Independent*, *Kaleidoscope* and *Time Out* before taking up his present job as artistic director of Battersea Arts Centre in London. He recently directed *Trio* and *All That Fall*.

For further information contact:
BAC, Lavender Hill, Battersea, London SW11 5TF
(telephone 0171 223 6557, fax 0171 978 5207).

I'm in two different minds about what the perfect theatre building should be.

I'm inspired by the way theatres worked when they were really a central part of culture in London, in the Elizabethan age. They were purpose-built to a market-driven model and seem to have worked incredibly well. But the most innovative work in London over the last twenty years or so has evolved in a very different economic environment, when purpose-built theatres have no longer been at the core of what has happened.

So in one sense my perfect theatre is an Elizabethan theatre that seems to have been built as an instrument in response to what was happening inside it, and on the other hand my perfect theatre is any space that artists arrive in like pirates and turn into a performance space.

Right. Is what you admire about it Elizabethan model the function of it, its role within that culture-
There's a lot of romantic conjecture about what an Elizabethan playhouse was like. There's no doubt that in terms of its place in the culture it was far closer to a warehouse being used for raves in King's Cross than the present National Theatre. Maybe there's a link there with modern site-specific work.

Theatres were built and theatre activity went on in places that were called the liberties, because they were outside the City of London and its jurisdiction. These were places possessed by people who weren't accommodated within the rules of society, that people went to in order to break those rules. Everyone knows that there were prostitutes and animal-baiting arenas just near the theatres, but we quickly jump into our romantic idea of what an Elizabethan playhouse was without thinking through what that means. There was a real sense of transgression about the act of going to the theatre.

It appears that it was full - it certainly made money - and it appears that the vast part of audiences were skiving from work, otherwise they couldn't possibly be there. I think piracy is a very important element in real creativity: a sense of seeping between the cracks in the framework of society and breaking the rules that everyone else is obeying. I actually think that that's central to why people go to the theatre, and it's central to the role of art.

People like to go to the theatre or a circus or a rave or a rock concert in order to come close to people and to an experience which is not obeying the same social rules that they are. To put it very crudely, we all make a certain number of compromises in order to take our place in whatever social structures we live in - and part of the attraction of live theatre or any live performance experience is the feeling that we're seeing someone who's not doing that. All the mythology about actors being mad and artists being close to madness, lunatics, lovers and poets being of imagination all compact - all of those little tricks in our language about what art is - to me indicate something very serious about why we're attracted to it.

We want artists to be mad?

We slightly resent our own compromises to normality so we like to be reminded of the possibility of not making those compromises and the possibility of living in a freer environment.

It's a cliché that we're attracted to icons because they live dangerously but that's a very important point for me. Phelim McDermott having the extraordinary courage to develop a piece of theatre which at least *seems* to be nakedly honest to its audience is living just as dangerously as James Dean, but in a different way. The attraction is the same. If you're watching *70 Hill Lane* part of it is "My God, I can't believe that he is daring to be so honest."

At the moment the whole arts industry is in a state of rabbit-like bewilderment because of the National Lottery. It is comic to see arts administrators running around in a state of confusion because our very identity is made out of an environment of hardship, shortage, blarney and ideological cant: "Save theatre!" - "Why?"

To suddenly have the government say: We're going to release this money and build your ideal theatre is very confusing. Because I think there's a great danger that we'll just say: "Right, what sort of building would I like? I'd like a theatre with every possible technical convenience and the combined wisdom of a generation of theatre architechts the way theatres have been built in Germany for years."

Interestingly the Germans are now in a recession. The theatres there are suddenly having to go through the kind of processes which happened here in the eighties.

The important point is that in Germany a history of lavish funding has nourished a completely different culture of creativity and no doubt a rich one, but we're not part of that. The really interesting work here in Britain over the last 20 years has developed through shortage and the kinds of improvisation and inspiration that are the result of shortage. In building the theatres of the future we have to be very careful to support the culture which really exists, not the culture we think should exist.

This is *not* an argument against funding for the arts. I was talking to Tim Barlow of Theatre de Complicite about *More Bigger Snacks Now* which won the Perrier Award in whatever it was... 1986. They had a surreal lighting cue, a central pool of light in a bedsit where it was set. Tim Barlow said "We were rehearsing in a basement in London and the only light came from this glass hole in the pavement above us. Inevitably we found ourselves working around it and that became a key part of the show."

So when they toured it-

They had to put it in the lighting design. The kind of dialogue that artists have had with spaces that aren't built as theatres have (a) made artists' lives very difficult but (b) been the source of lots of kinds of inspiration which I think have been very rich.

And in an environment now when theatre's main problem is to say to people: Come to the theatre, don't watch recorded art, don't watch telly or don't watch film-

Or record it and watch it later.

That sense of poverty of resource is a real strength. Again Phelim McDermott is an artist who's fresh in my mind because we've just had *70 Hill Lane* here, but the whole basis of that show is him talking to an audience and saying: "Well, you know we don't have this but imagine it... I'm just going to put some sellotape here, imagine it's a house." There's no way that he can build a house in the theatre in the way that he could in a film.

When theatre goes down the route of trying to provide a complete imitation of life - as it did in the nineteenth century and to an extent earlier in this century - it was able to do so because it was technologically the most advanced way of doing that. Now it isn't. So it's got to do something else. So when Phelim McDermott says to an audience: I can't do this, can you imagine it? that's the strength. That is why people should want to go to the theatre - not to be given a complete art object to take home.

And, by coincidence, what's the best analogy to that? The prologue to *Henry V.*

Yes!

A guy comes on stage and says: Sorry we haven't got any horses, we haven't got any of these, but when we say this, can you just imagine? - and you saw them. It's the same. Precisely the reason that audiences do enjoy coming to the theatre rather than watching a film is because the product they see is *unfinished*. It is incomplete and it doesn't work unless they creatively complete it.

Watching theatre is a creative act in the same way that listening to the radio is a creative act, or that reading a book is a creative act - because the poverty of the medium is explicit. There's this ludicrous thing about a member of the audience at *Cats* trying to sue -

For false imprisonment.
Because the Rum Tum Tugger was wobbling his groin in her face. And (*smiles*) obviously I don't want to prejudice those proceedings but Charles Spencer - God bless him - wrote a piece in the *Daily Telegraph* about this in which he said something like we go to the theatre to be entertained, not to be part of the entertainment. Wrong, Charlie! That's why you go to a film.
For me crucially audiences *are* part of the entertainment. Not because everyone else is laughing at a single member of the audience - which is what he meant and why he *does* have a point - but because the performance is incomplete without an audience.

It might be interesting to talk about strategies for dealing with poverty.
But the other problem is strategies for dealing with *riches*. That's the problem for the nineties. What will happen when all the money that has poured into Lottery projects becomes visible?
That's a separate problem from the disgrace that the Lottery money has gone to buildings and not to artists.

It's a subsidy to the construction industry essentially.
Yes, but the key thing that was needed and that continues to be needed is to give artists the resources in terms of *food* and *drink* to respond creatively to the places where they might make their work. Obviously the better equipped theatres are the better it is for theatre, but that's happened the wrong way round.
And the danger of it happening the wrong way round is that one of the first things to go in our brave new theatres might be those very unaccountable, bizarre, surprising spaces within which that open-minded collaboration between artists and audience can most easily happen. The element of surprise, of ambush, is crucial. Sometimes audiences forget how involved they can be. Sometimes *we* forget, running a building, the staff who work here. We've got 1700 performances in a year. It's very easy to forget that it's all about creative involvement of the audience (*laughs*) and just imagine that it's about getting the next load of troublesome artists through the door.

And out again.
That element of surprise - and the creativity which it brings about on the part of an audience - is never something that you can settle with. Once you've done it once, you have to do it again and again and again, you can't just say: Right, that's it, I've got my surprising formula sorted out now. It stops being surprising.

An example of this occurred during the *British Festival of Visual Theatre* last October. We had quite a diverse programme, and in the middle of it we had an artist called Andrew Bailey, who had previously worked on the stand-up circuit as a character called The Great Podomovsky. He wanted to do something, we didn't have any resources, so we basically had him running all over the building, and he did a guided tour.

There were all sorts of obstacles to this like Health and Safety rules. You were not allowed to take people down to the cellar. If you're taking people into the courtyard there, a slate fell off the roof in 1984 so people need to wear hard hats... And every single material and administrative obstacle that he encountered as an artist he piratically conquered and integrated into the show. Once we'd had this hard hat conversation, we thought: "Oh no" and he just said: "Fantastic, brilliant, all the audience wear hard hats." So throughout the theatre there were these lines of people wandering through the building wearing orange hard hats with Wandsworth Council written on the front. And audiences who'd come for other shows were coming up, saying: "What the hell is going on here?"

Then, without asking us, he started painting white paint over the inside of our courtyard - which was a problem with our landlords. And I said: "Andrew, I'm afraid you're going to have to remove it." And he said: "Oh, it's not a problem, I want to have these characters as monks wandering around behind the audience all the time. We could have them sandpapering the walls as a kind of pennance - and by the end of the run it will be clean."

His work was underresourced and chaotic. And I want to find the resources through lottery A4E, the new fund which is going to enable us to spend some money on work and artists, to enable him to do something that is more organized and a more polished product. But I have to remember all of the advantages that came out of that weird improvisational dialogue with the building and with us when there were no resources. And I have to try and protect that in the new resourced environment that I want him to work in.

The theatre we're in here was built as a town hall, and it's very expensive just to have it open. Its theatre spaces weren't built as theatre spaces and its non-theatre spaces obviously are rather grand; a marble staircase, glass mosaic floor, stained glass domed foyer and all this stuff, which are explicitly untheatrical. When we started talking to our architects about what we should do with Lottery money for the building, the temptation was to say; we'll have three perfectly proportioned well-equipped black box theatres with everything you could wish for - that's what we've been waiting for in the arts for years and years.

But the more that I turn the theatre spaces here into archetypal black boxes, the less reason there is for anyone to come here rather than go anywhere else. And the more opportunities for that real sense of counterpoint between that work and the building - which makes work special, alive and distinctive for the artist and the audience - will be missing.

It's important that theatres are distinctive and one of the problems in London is that they aren't. Theatre takes place in places not theatres - or interesting theatre does. And in my mind the distinctive atmosphere of the place is more important than the design of the theatre, though I understand that the two can be related.

My favourite theatre in London is the Theatre Royal in Stratford East, and that's largely because it's distinctive. When you go there, there is an extraordinarily strong atmosphere, there is a real sense of relationship between the audience and what happens on stage, which is achieved through subsidy - no other way - and which permeates every aspect of the architecture of the place from the Matcham design of the auditorium to the bar. Making that step is the key challenge for what I would call real theatre spaces in London. The West End is set up to work on a different basis, a free market, but real theatres have to develop their atmosphere in collaboration with their audience and have to develop their audience through that ongoing thing.

Does it help to know why you're going to the theatre?

I go to see what's live and exciting - that's my criterion really, whether something is live culture or not, which is very difficult to define. Frantic Assembly, The Clod Ensemble are theatre companies whose work meets with a mixed response from critics. But the critical response is irrelevant because even without a massive marketing budget people come and see it. People respond to something that's happening in it. And I think they do that because there's nothing reiterative about what those artists are doing, whether there are mistakes in it or not it's genuinely growing. It's extraordinary how reliant theatre is on the press.

Is this one of the imperfections of theatre as it exists at the moment?

One of the imperfections is that it's *too* reliant. What tends to happen now is that a theatre show goes on and then it either happens or not as a cultural event depending on what the press say. And I think that makes for conservative theatre, really. It's not an easy problem to solve but what I would like to happen is for something to be happening and for the media to discover it rather than for something to happen because the media say it should.

In the *British Festival of Visual Theatre* for example last October we had a lot of work that was on for two nights by artists whose work is not very well known. There was precious little press for it but audiences were extremely high because artists knew their work was going on in a clear context and that there was other related work going on around it so you could get a word of mouth and their natural cultures could grow together.

And they could also see each other's work and meet each other, get drunk afterwards and stuff.
Yes.

That works fine with a small theatre but what about somewhere bigger? How many seats does a perfect theatre have?
I think there's a very important place for small theatres. It shouldn't cost any less to pay six actors who work in a small theatre than it does to pay six actors who work in a 1300-seater. But the mere constraint of size means that when you're doing your budgets, everyone is aware, your funders are aware, your audience is aware, the artists are aware that there's not a huge commercial risk attached to the work. That does mean that you can really experiment. And I think audiences respond to that. Quite a lot of the work that we've put on here, particularly in Studio 2, is actually presented to the audience as an experiment, so part of the liveness of the experience for the audience is that they know they are seeing something that is working itself out and that they are part of that.

There's a lot of nonsense talked about small-scale theatre in London and the London fringe taking the place of rep - some of it by me (*laughs*). That's never an argument for not funding rep theatres, but I think it's incontrovertibly true that some artists have found places to experiment and develop on a small scale in London who might otherwise have gone through the rep system if it was funded properly. And that work has taken place in unaccountable spaces like the gallery in Spitalfields where Primitive Science did the first version of *Primitive Librarian* - because there's no normal theatre environment to accommodate that.

There's also a huge amount of cant around at the moment about consultation. We have the extraordinary spectacle of both political parties making policy through market research. And there's a bit of a pressure through the redevelopment of the theatre for us to go the same way, for us to put out endless questionnaires and ask people what they want and try and give it to them. And I think there's a big danger there. Your relationship with your audience in that process becomes a bit like a relationship between two lovers when one of them says: What would *you* really like to do? and the other says: No, what would *you* really like to do? - the kind of relationship you end up trying to bust your head out of from sheer boredom: an absolute nightmare.

It's vital for arts organizations to grasp the fact that their role is to *lead*. Their role is to have a genuine dialogue with their audience, but a dialogue which begins with them in a charismatic role saying: Come on! Join us!

Offering inspiration.

The starting point is not fawning consultation. It's inspiration and conviction, which I believe leads to the kind of relationship with an audience of the kind that you have in Stratford East, and that's the most vital ingredient in a theatre.

Some of the most interesting kinds of theatre work I've seen or heard about recently are taking place in the streets. Teatr Biuro Podrozy for example made an extraordinary lament for the war in Bosnia which involved stiltwalkers and fire and the language of street carnival but the sensibility of tragic theatre. It was extraordinary the way that people were able to watch it and the concentration people were able to bring to it.

This is theatre that people can stumble across by accident without necessarily intending to go looking for it?

Yes, I think that the clearest way to get that creative involvement from an audience is to have some sense of ambush, some sense of surprise. It's a bit like the way in which you can fall in love when you're on holiday.

(Laughs.)

Or you can fall in love through a completely chance meeting in an unlikely place. Because if you're on holiday you've planned to be open, given yourself a kind of licence. But sometimes you can be interrupted and find yourself completely uninhibited. So part of what we need to do as a theatre is to invite people to choose to go to the liberties, the place where Shakespeare's theatre was, to choose to escape in one way or another, and to be open creatively as well. But if enough people aren't doing that, then we can surprise people.

And that might mean a number of insititutions taking the Lottery money that's available, creating some very well-equipped, nice, comfortable, safe spaces and then not using them.

Yeah. Well, I don't know what's going to happen to those big re-equipped theatres. I think essentially they're about a different sort of culture from what we're about here. We've got a different role, partly because of scale and partly because of growth. The whole point of what goes on here is that it's growing.

Does that mean it needs somewhere else to grow to?

That's a good point. It can carry on growing here, but there's a danger that it becomes like an ingrowing toenail.

And presumably there are other people at an earlier stage in their development whom you want to give the space to?

We're just reassessing and trying to formalise how we find the next people.

People say that theatre is a middle-class pursuit - and it is. One of the main reasons for that is that in order to get your foot on the first rung you have to get a show on in a small venue on the fringe in London. Basically that's the route. In order to do that, you have to raise between five and seven thousand pounds. Until now that has meant that the directors who can do that either have resources from their family and friends that they can call on or they are very persuasive fundraisers. Some of those people are also very good directors, but an ability to raise money is by no means the best criterion for selecting who your best directors are. Now the new A4E Lottery fund has just decided to give out lots of five thousand pounds to anyone who asks. It's a splattergun response to that problem, but maybe it will help. Part of what I see as our responsibility here is to help people over that first step.

What I would like is for this building to be seen as a development space at any point in someone's career. It already happens that artists go from here on tour or to the South Bank or to the West End or to the National and that kind of through journey is very important. But what's more important is that rather than try to put the lid on those artists and stop them going anywhere else, if they want to try something out later on in their career then they come back here. Hopefully development and growth aren't things that stop once you reach a certain point. Harry Hill has grown through and beyond BAC in terms of the audiences he's able to command, but when he's got some new ideas he wants to try out he just comes here and does them in a studio for whoever turns up, forty people, because that's the way he likes his work to grow. And it's very important to me, that people come back because of that environment.

Does this mean the perfect theatre also contains the possibility of failure?

I hate the phrase "the right to fail". Not because I think that all programming should be conservative but because it makes no accommodation for the audience. It betrays an essentially masturbatory understanding of art. Whatever right there is to experiment and for something not to work, it relates to a process that involves an audience as well as artists. I don't expect every show that comes here to be absolutely brilliant, but I never expect artists to think they have a right to fail their audience. Even if a show doesn't work, it must include the audience in some way.

And do you think that in a way it's a valuable and necessary part of the audience experience that it doesn't always work equally well, that you can't tell before you've seen something whether it's really-

I don't think you're ever going to persude people to go to theatre on the basis that it might be bad, but people go and watch their football team and they know they might lose.

They know they're taking a calculated risk and they know what the broad dynamics of that risk are.

Theatre is a different thing, but there is something of the same kind of quality of relationship that I think theatre needs. I want people to come here because of the way in which things happen here, because of the kind of involvement that they feel from the building and the work that they see - and if they like something less than the thing they saw last week then that's not the end of the story.

It's very important for me that we have no green room here. If you were building a theatre from scratch you could have a separate artists' entrance, a separate artists' staircase, a separate artists' bar and a separate artists' exit. Artists and audiences here come in through the same door, they drink in the same bar, they eat in the same café and that's very important from the point of view of the nature of collaboration I want artists and audience to have. I don't think that all theatres should not have a green room or not have a stage door, I just think that *this* theatre shouldn't have those things. Because it's not a theatre, it's given the opportunity to create a different kind of relationship which is distinctive and productive

Marc von Henning
Theatre Dream

Marc von Henning was born in 1960, in London. He translates, writes and directs for theatre. *Theatremachine*, his translations of theatre texts by the late German playwright Heiner Müller is published by Faber & Faber. For *primitive science* he has written and directed *Hunger*, *Spell* and *Primitive Librarian*, all performed at the Young Vic Theatre (1995-97). His latest theatre text, *After the Hunt*, is published in Performance Research. He lives and works in London.

Contact: c/o *primitive science*,
4-5 Lamb Street, Spitalfields, London E1 6EA
(telephone/fax. 0171 247 9745).

> *Man has known, since antiquity, that in dreams he encounters what he is and what he will be, what he has done and what he is going to do, discovering there the knot that ties his freedom to the necessity of the world.*
> **Foucault**

A stage. Stripped of the fickle costume of ideas, it l
naked and abandoned as a stormed palace. Its darkn
is barely spoiled by a dull light, though there can be
hiding the evidence of recent activity: a haze
perspiration, tired echoes of applause, the petals o
flower, carnation rose lily, crushed into the flo
boards. Remnants of a ritual I cannot remember taki
part in. The dream, so it seems, began without me a
now that the play is over, the players have retreate
the auditorium empty but for a handful of babbli
stragglers, it finds me, by coincidence surely, in t
wings of the theatre. Why I didn't leave with t
others, is hard to say. It is late, midnight at lea
Unlikely that I should have been entrusted to perfor
a task at this hour. Then again, why am I dressed in
uniform, too long in the sleeves, and borrowed boo
In my right hand, it trembles gently, an envelope, t
address smudged, probably by the sweat from n
palm. I am, or have lately been, nervous. Perhaps I a
an actor. Of course, I am an actor, and earlier on t
evening I missed my entrance, dozed off on the jo
lost in a day-dream. My part: a messenger, due
enter, out of breath, in the short scene just before t
battle, a scene often cut from production and replace
by a soft whisper in the emperor's ear. I have nothi
to say, my duty simple: the delivery of a letter, the o
now rotting between my fingers. Tonight my part w
have been played by a machine. A rudimentary devi
attached to the grid which, when operated, releases
rolled-up parchment as though it were being droppe
from the sky by a bird, king of the messengers. Or els
my failure to arrive was obscured by slight but swi
adjustment to the lighting. Either way, my absen
went unnoticed. Except, of course, by my employer
they will not overlook the incident. My already pet
future in this profession will end sooner than I though
I make for the exit, but the long walk across the no
decidedly colder stage is interrupted. Sniggering an
whispers in the stalls. The arrival of a second audienc
must have passed me by. I was after all absorbed i
confusion. Now, the house is full. Hardly typic
theatre clientele, though. Some perched on the bac

of their seats, others slouching in the aisles, caresses and fisticuffs in the gallery, wolf-whistling children on shoulders, ball games, snoring fathers slumped across mothers' laps. The attire is a frenzied medley of accoutrements from half a dozen centuries and no adequate separation between lords gentlemen commoners peasants. THE GARDEN OF EDEN WAS A JUNGLE. Apart from that, my eyes, otherwise weak and flawed, cannot help but see through their bodies as they would through a flimsy silk gown, or shallow fog. At times I have an almost clear view of the red velvet upholstering on the seats behind. My ears are less fortunate; for all the brouhaha I see, the only sound is the sniggering and whispers from the stalls. These creatures, there can be little doubt, are not of this world, nor are my two new stage companions who also seem to have appeared in a moment's distraction. A woman, standing close, almost behind me, mimes smoking a cigarette. A man paces about waving a stick. At me? Have I been expected here? Both are wearing masks, the only impenetrable part of their anatomies; his, a dark, kind yet solemn face, her's, a younger, almost vicious grin, father and daughter perhaps. The man spreads his arms out at me, a welcome gesture - the stick already no more than a faint memory. I try to resist, but curiosity, the strongest of the vices, conquers my composure and in an attempt to embrace him, I tumble through his shape and onto the ground. Out of the corner of my eye I see the audience in stitches, unable to contain themselves. Of course, I am in the company of ghosts, performing to the dead of night, the live buffoon in an otherwise tragic scene. I have been made a laughing stock, but what really compels the onlookers is that the envelope, so crucial to my former existence, has been manoeuvred from my clenched fist. The man/magician holds it up for the crowd to see. They hail his accomplishment, and while the woman beckons me to rise from the floor and join her, he opens the letter. But rather than use his eyes on it, he begins to stroke the script with his fingertips, then holds it to his nose and sniffs at it. Ah, the perfume of patience. Now he knows me. His admirers await another trick. He puts the letter to his lips. GHOSTS WILL DRINK KISSES FROM MY PAGES was Kafka's dream. I'd not have guessed it would come true in mine. As though an instinctive conclusion to the act, he begins to eat the letter, stuffing it whole into his mouth before chewing and swallowing. To my surprise, the audience do not find this amusing, but are riveted to the edges of their seats. Even the sniggering and whispers have died down, all eyes on the hero. In the silence that is perfect theatre he slowly collapses to the ground and pales into insignificance. A masterful exit. One by one the audience rise to their feet, though the chant I read from their lips is not ENCORE but MURDERER MURDERER, the standing ovation of a lynch mob. Excitement shifts to fear. No use explaining that I am only the messenger and not to blame if the letter or its words turn out to be poisoned. And how can I be accused of killing a ghost. I look around, maybe my other undead stage companion can advise me, but she too has vanished, leaving in her place a golden goblet, around it an echo in the voice of my wife: DO YOU WANT TO DRINK MY BLOOD. I hold the goblet up to the disgruntled crowd. A salute they obey with calm. I take my time, sipping swigging drinking down the sweet red sap. A final solo, as it turns out, for the moment I'm done the auditorium lies empty. This breed of spectator does not, of course, leave row by row, but disappears in the bat of an eye. No concern for lengthy ceremonies of appreciation. I bow to no one. From somewhere IN THE GODS a blinding gleam of what must be new daylight. The hours - what is time in the presence of ghosts - have flown by. The dream leaves me in the wings which I know now to be my home.

David Farr & Rose Garnett
Showing the Truth

David Farr and Rose Garnett are artistic director and producer of The Gate Theatre in Notting Hill, London.

For further information contact:
Gate Theatre, 11 Pembridge Road, London W11 3HQ
(telephone 0171 229 5387, fax 0171 221 6055)

Do you want the theatre to be perfect?

DAVID: When you go to see theatre I don't think you can ever lose sig
of the imperfections or the roughness of what you have in front of yo
Having said that, I also think it can be a holy experience. And ho
experience implies hope towards something perfect or sublime. Tha
perhaps, is what I would aim for. It's probably a better definition
perfection.

If you are living in a fairly irreligious and unspiritual world, i
difficult to reconcile that with constantly trying to produce spiritual ar
holy pieces of work. They threaten to lose their worldliness and the
wisdom and their use. So my work is often quite deliberately ugly ar
unaesthetic and clashes with conventional ideas of harmony and perfectio
But fundamentally I want to produce something that is in some wa
beautiful and sacred.

And for you the theatre is a way of seeking these qualities-

DAVID: Yes, without doubt.

One among many or is it unique?

DAVID: It is the only one *for me*. The reason it has that quality is as muc
to do with the making and the doing of it as with the witnessing of i
Theatre is the only art form where when you go and see something yo
still feel as if you are part of the making of it. Most other media are on
about the result. There's something quite magical at times about the actu
process and experience of getting to somewhere, a theatre, which is ver
releasing.

My favourite feeling in the theatre is that when you go in there yo
can still feel the presence of all the work that came before. That
something you also get in religious spaces - that feeling of rituals whic
still ring around in the space. That's wonderful. If some of them a
anarchic, some of them are pagan, some of them are intensely orthodo
some of them are very tragic and some of them are comic, that can becom
very exciting. But ultimately the kind of theatre I'm talking about is a ver
serious business about love and death and all those things.

**And is part of that dealing with life and death and related issues th
transience of the theatrical form itself? Does that link up with valuing th
ability to change from one theatre to another, to be able as a directo
someone creating theatre, to be able to go into a different space which h.
its own history, which has a tradition of a certain kind of work an
suddenly enter into some sort of dialogue with that?**

DAVID: It's not really where my heart lies. My favourite thing would l
to find a space I'm very attached to and then stay there for ever.

A nest?

DAVID: Yes, definitely. And to be able to bring other people into that and see what happens to them. That's my dream. I'm not that interested in buying into different identities all the time. I'm not that flexible in experimenting with my style and thinking I can try a bit of this and try a bit of that. So I think my real desire would be to do the opposite: to find somewhere I could bring people who have similar ideas-

But not exactly the same-

DAVID: A similar - I like the word "seriousness".

Are disgreements one of the things that can keep a theatre alive?

DAVID: A lot of powermongering is thinly disguised by a patina of ideological debate that isn't really true. There is a part of theatre that worries me that is just one step from politics - people who should really be in politics and are fundamentally interested in the mechanisms of power. I find the connection between theatre and power really interesting and the history of it. There are people who can get a lot of power somehow, miraculously, through doing plays, which I find astounding. I'm a bit suspicious sometimes of attitudes that might just be convenient at this moment and might be switched quite happily about two years later. I've seen that happen a couple of times.

Can you give any examples of that?

DAVID: When I started at the Gate there was a famous kind of long running rivalry between the Bush and the Gate, as to which work was more useful or more useless. In fact it's a completely absurd question. And I wanted to try and break that barrier down. That's one of the reasons that I've introduced British writers into the Gate, to say that there is actually rather an important connection between British writing now and European classical writing then. There is an interesting argument about the place of British writing within the European classical tradition. What is not interesting is a sort of value judgement about whether it is more important to go and see a Lope de Vega play this week than it is to go and see a play by Richard Cameron.

In London at the moment all the theatres at whatever level within the funded sector are trying to create an identity for themselves which is distinct and separate from the others. However, the criterion for distinguishing between theatres has become one of form: this is where you go to see a text by a living writer rehearsed for three weeks, this is where you go to see plays by people who've never written a play before, this is where you go to see work which has been devised by a group of people... rather than a philosophical perspective or any more fundamental sense of what theatre does.

ROSE: (*Arrives.*) Hi, David.

DAVID: One of the things which becomes more apparent to us as our funding increases from having been zero to now approaching near poverty is the more money you get, the more you have to explain your niche - that's quite literally the word - in terms of what you are doing for London, or what you are doing for Britain. If we say we are London's centre of international drama it is very clearly understandable to any member of the London Arts Board what that means. It contains within it implications that you're thinking of doing lots of different types of theatre: you're trying to represent one day an Eastern style of theatre - how do you represent an Indian theatre piece in English with English actors? - and the next day you're looking at a German tradition or a French.

Is there a utopian dimension to this internationalism, of wanting to represent other cultures on something more like their own terms by doing plays like - well some plays in the last Biennale season for example?

DAVID: The Biennale was undertaken with the knowledge that at least some of those shows were not going to "work" in a conventional sense. It's quite interesting to see which of those break through into an English forum and which don't - sometimes it's just to do with how well they're done, other times it's to do with more deep problems. That season is a really important part of what we're doing and we're going to repeat it because it's about saying that sometimes you have to do work that is not necessarily going to be understood *now* but will actually drip through into the culture in some way and have an effect *eventually*. There are a lot of great theatrical successes at that moment and they're not remembered at all.

So your perfect theatrical experience goes beyond instant gratification - maybe it requres a more protracted emotional and intellectual process to come to terms with it?

DAVID: Yeah, I do think it's possible for a theatre to become a centre for proper thinking and debate. That's ultimately quite an intellectual, snobbish position to take, but I think theatre is able to argue about things on quite a refined level. It can actually change people's opinions about things, not necessarily through rational argument or through emotional

blackmail-
ROSE: But by showing the truth.
DAVID: Yeah.

What do you need to do that, to show the truth?
ROSE: I think at the moment you need a small theatre, sadly.
DAVID: Probably.
ROSE: Our big luxury is that we can have much wider parameters than somebody who's catering for four hundred, and they can have wider parameters than somebody who's catering for a thousand. Hopefully our pushing the parameters means we're part of a chain. So Botho Strauss was on at the RSC last year after being on here four years ago.
Despite all the practical nightmares which we have financially - we can't always find the directors and the actors which we'd in an ideal world like to use because we can't offer them the same kind of rewards that they want at the moment - we exchange that for extraordinary luxuries in the type of work that we can put on.
DAVID: I think if you really want to create a theatre rather than just a theatre experience - but a building that is constantly producing work which has that kind of significance I think it can do - then you have to be asking people to come here who have to have a serious passion and belief that they have some truth to tell.

Is that in a way an advantage of working at the Gate where you're not able to pay people as they would be paid in larger theatres, that their motivation becomes a much more evident factor?
ROSE: I don't think not paying people is ever an advantage. I really mind not paying people.

I wasn't suggesting that you didn't.
ROSE: What it often means is that for people with genuine motives, who at the same time are past the point where they always want to be paid for their work, coming to the Gate is a harder decision than it should be. So it means that we lose people, not that we gain better motives.
DAVID: Ideally people would want to come here because they realise that something's going on that they want to be involved with. It's a credit I think to the theatre that even without paying them there are some people come here for that reason. We also have to realise that some people come here because they'll get noticed. What would be perfect would be to have everybody coming to a space because of the work and the sequence of work that is being offered, that they want to be part of that communal experience.
I think it's very difficult these days to get a communality going in any form of life. Everything is so transitory. Actors are like products, they move

around and it's very hard to hold anyone down. It's very difficult to get repertory companies going and all this sort of stuff. But I think in a funny way the way to do it is not to *pretend* that you can get those huge structures like in Germany. In England I think what you have to do instead is celebrate the whole chaotic nature of the whole thing: celebrate the fact that people do come and go, that there is a constantly changing workforce, a constantly changing stream of ideas, a constantly changing stream of artists, but something remains true and fixed which somehow means that that doesn't become random or arbitrary, that there is in each piece of work a continuity from the last.

That puts a great responsibility on programming to be able to inspire that level of commitment and application.

DAVID: It also puts a responsibility on developing relationships with certain people who will return or, if not return, have an influence. A lot of people in their thirties are crying out for something. They don't necessarily want to do every project. They want to help, they want to give suggestions, they want to have an idea for something that someone else might do.

ROSE: They want a *home*, that's what people really desire - a place where they are accepted and comfortable, where they don't have to sell their ideas. And that's what a community does - your ideas are valid. Even if they're not used they'll be given space. And we have lots of people like that here, which is nice. Even though they might not have directed here for a long time or acted here for a long time, they're still part of the fluid nature of the place.

DAVID: If we continue to do work which is in some way engaging with what theatre is, asking what is it? what can it be? - then that kind of group will stay around and people will continue to be interested.

To engage with what theatre is - does that mean that you expect the people that come here as members of the audience to already have seen another kind of theatre before they come? Do you see yourselves as a theatre for a slightly more refined kind of audience?

DAVID: Anyone coming into the theatre, even if they've never been to a theatre before, might be surprised at what theatre can do. International work can do that but it can also be done with an English play - Gregory Motton's play *cat & mouse (sheep)* is probably as challenging a thing about what theatre is as any we've done. The irony is that people find it much easier to understand the strangeness of a foreign piece than to understand the strangeness of a piece written close to home.

ROSE: They give a foreign play many more permissions than they give a British play. Foreign plays are allowed to be tangential or difficult in a way that here is too uncomfortable; it becomes weird rather than exotic.

DAVID: Also you know that Motton is writing something close to home but you can't quite work out what it is.
ROSE: People find it much more intimidating.

Do you like that about the theatre?
ROSE: No, but I don't mind it either. The only thing that I mind is that self-satisfaction people get from going to the theatre. I think most people go to the theatre now, particularly somewhere like the National or West End straight plays, for reasssurance. They like just enough reassurance so they come out feeling clever that they've got it. That's why Stoppard or Shaffer are so immensely successful. Even though they think they're asking questions, I find them an oddly reassuring presence.

The answers are never that far away.
ROSE: Exactly. People know that if they'd thought a bit they would have got there themselves. So they come out having a fairly self-satisfied, complacent night at the theatre for all the reasons they think they haven't had a complacent night at the theatre.
And so intimidation is not a bad thing - as long as a play is giving access at some point, even if it denies it later on a bit.
DAVID: There is a kind of test which is to do with the heart. I am always looking for work that somehow has a real conviction behind it. Sometimes it's delightful if that conviction is utterly apparent and stated in the work. That was the attraction of something like *The Boat Plays*. You're looking at a completely certain system of belief that is totally alien and discredited. Suddenly it makes you think: Maybe my system of belief is equally discredited, maybe my system of beliefs is equally up for grabs. That's fascinating.
Then there are writers like Strindberg, like Valle Inclan, who are what I would call restless writers. I have a great attraction personally to these kinds of writers, for whom any kind of faith is very, very hard. And yet somewhere underneath they really want to find it.

I think it's very interesting that your view of the ideal theatre you want to create includes contributions from people who are dead - in some cases long and extremely dead. Because there is a countervaling movement which always suggests that the theatre is live, present, lived experience, and the ultimate in theatrical experience has to be the perfect experience of the present moment and what's happening now.
DAVID: There's no doubt at all that I personally think very much in terms of traditions, in terms of heritages, and I believe if you can create a sense of communality or a sense of movement, even informally, then that will have a very powerful legacy which people can pick up on for many years and that's exciting. Placing writers in a tradition helps audiences understand

the connections as well, helps them understand a more expansive view of what theatre and what life can be. I'd like to think if someone came to see a year's worth of Gate plays - in a *good* year -

(*Laughs.*) **You can choose the year.**
DAVID: That would be a very enhancing experience. Seeing all those different things, they would add up to something. What's very odd is that we seem to get a remarkably different set of people for an Indian play compared with a German play - and that's a strange thing to reconcile with trying to find a unifying vision for the whole thing.

Do you think theatre is something that can still be a valuable and useful ingredient in everybody's life or are there inevitably only going to be a certain section of the population who are interested in theatre?
DAVID: Interesting question.

Because if the ideal theatre is a small one which has say ten people on stage and seventy in the audience does that mean that to cover the entire poulation of London there needs to be 100,000 theatres?
ROSE: I don't know, is that the ideal theatre?
DAVID: No, I don't feel it's the ideal theatre.
ROSE: It's just got a very important place.
DAVID: My ideal theatre was something that would have this atmosphere hopefully in a bigger space. But even having said that, it would only be 300 - it's not 3,000. By its very nature it's impossible, of course it is, for theatres to have an effect on every single member of the population, and I think that's why the populist argument is a strange one. Because you know there is only a finite number of people you can communicate with with one theatre piece at one time. A show at the National can only communicate to sixty or seventy thousand, something like that, whereas a film... in theory everyone can see it.

I suppose what I'm thinking of is more: Is it important for people who aren't going to the theatre to know that it's there, to know that they might be able to go if they wanted to?
DAVID: Yes, it's extremely important. A much more difficult argument than the London argument where the access is really very good is the argument to do with-
ROSE: Should somebody in Bradford subsidize the National Theatre?
DAVID: If this sort of work is interesting and valuable, why is it only taking place in one city? That's why it's important that there are other theatres like this. I don't think that trying to tour the work that we do is necessarily very helpful because part of the experience is coming to here, to our place. I think there have to be other small theatres, trying to have the same kind of ideas and ambitions all over the country.

Do you actually need a city of 8 million people maybe in order to be able to have a theatre of this size doing this kind of work?
DAVID: I don't think that's true. No. Because I think the smaller a city is the more interest there is in what's happening in it. I think the work would have to be different, but work with a similar kind of intention is absolutely possible, definitely.
ROSE: The thing that a really good theatre or an enlightened theatre can do is that they can educate their audience. That's where I sometimes get resentful of the way the people at the National run the Cottesloe: they're not fulfilling the obligation of the small theatre to put on work which edges people along.

It has the problem that it is run by an organization which is consistently preoccupied with the process of putting on theatre in a larger space and therefore finds it very difficult to pick up on a different set of criteria.
ROSE: But then I think they should make a different set of claims. What I dislike about it is it's making claims which it's not fulfilling.
DAVID: It would be very exciting for a small space like that to have really a separate programming entirely.

Do you think ideally a management should only have one space at their disposal? Maybe it's actually a mistake to have more than one space.
DAVID: I think it is. The problem of the Studio theatre - the idea that it's just the Young Vic *studio* or the Lyric Hammersmith *studio* -
ROSE: It's the problem of the second division.
DAVID: Fundamentally I think a theatre is about a space - and it is going to be dictated by *one* space. That makes somewhere like the Almeida potentially a perfect set-up; it is one space, in theory a beautiful space, and it has all the possibilities. There's nothing more unenjoyable than going to a theatrical building which just has nothing going for it. You walk in and it's just a prefabricated black nastiness somebody has been forced to put their show in - that is terrible, it's no way to see a play at all. And that's the difficulty with creating modern theatre buildings. It is very difficult to make those places receptive theatrical spaces.

Ideally you want something that looks like somewhere you've never been before?
DAVID: Somewhere that has an identity and crucially, if possible, has a history. If you can find a building that has a history and is theatrically a competent space to do with sightlines and to do with where the focus is on the stage I think that would be ideal. It doesn't have to be crumbling and old - everyone goes on about looking for old Bouffes du Nord sort of things.

Does a building with an evident history free up making theatre there - if a history's already there before you start you don't have to invent one? I got the sense when the Gate was redeveloped and the shape of it was completely changed, it was very difficult to recognize it as the place where I'd seen various shows before. And I thought certainly the first shows that were done when the building was reopened were in a way intended to remind you that it was still the same theatre.

DAVID: Yes, they were. That was a good example of a space being expanded and suddenly suffering for a while and having to refind its feet. It needed a year -

I think in fact you've been very successful in giving it a more familiar feel very quickly.

DAVID: Yeah, but it's taken a lot of effort from everyone. One of the first decisions we made when we first came here was to try and get people to realise that the space didn't work as it used to work. It needed whole new ways of thinking about it and, put simply, a much more environmental approach. And that's now become exciting, but you have to keep changing because you start to see replicas of other sets.

ROSE: Or the designers and directors suddenly feeling the pressure of invention, again doing things for the sake of it, rather than doing what the work dictates as necessary.

DAVID: The strange thing about our theatre is I don't think it's a particularly beautiful space. It's a slightly too long corridor. The expansion was only semi-successful. But you can make it into something successful. Maybe if you have an amazingly beautiful, stunning space maybe it oppresses some of the work or maybe it forces a certain aesthetic onto the work.

ROSE: You have the obligations of exploiting it. If you don't use something, you're missing an opportunity. The Gate is a difficult space, and the difficulties are apparent to the audience.

Does the apparentness of those constraints go together with your notion of truth?

DAVID: Yes, but I think the really interesting argument is: Is it possible to imagine this kind of theatre on a larger scale? That to me is a crucial question. There are lots and lots of things we'd like to do and can't. I'm not talking about choice of plays but choice of mode of production. Two things come particularly to mind - we can't do what I would call clean theatre here because it doesn't work. Our theatre *isn't* clean. And we also can't do much that involves the notion of distance. Everything has to be intimate and rough on a certain level, whether it be rough American naturalism and rough Portuguese poetic metaphor.

Is it possible to imagine a theatre which can have that rough, intimate thing and also has that notion of space which is something that I'm always kind of missing here? And then is it possible to run an organization which requires the kind of money to make a larger space work with the same kind of ideals we have here? And is it possible in London?

Ramin Gray
reports from Teheran

Ramin Gray is a freelance theatre director who has mainly worked
with contemporary playwrights such as Stephen Butchard,
Andrew Cullen, Paul Godfrey and Gregory Motton.
He has worked in London, Liverpool and Paris.

For further information contact:
138 Lancaster Road, London W11 1QU

I'm half-Iranian and going back there recently was a really important moment for me.

I hadn't been to Iran for 21 years, since I was a kid.

I'd always wondered why I ended up in theatre, maybe because I felt I didn't quite fit in as an English person and theatre is the home of all misfits. So when I got to Teheran I thought I should go and visit the theatre. Various people sent me along to a middle-class theatre where I saw a rather pretentious play with slightly radical, intellectual aspirations. Very boring. So I asked around a bit more. And eventually people said; Well if that's what you're interested in, you should probably go *downtown*.

Teheran is built on a slope. And all the rich people live up north with all the dregs draining down to the southern end. And I soon discovered that in Teheran theatre of quality gravitates downhill. This is where the bazaar is, the market where you can buy anything. It's all very bustling and thriving; this is an area where they sell car parts, spares for fridges, everything on earth, and there's all these men wandering around covered in grease - and it's really exciting. There's a street down there called Lalezar with a few rundown art deco theatre-cum-cinema buildings. Since its heyday in the Twenties and Thirties this area has become a bit seedy - not quite red light but verging on that - and before the Revolution the theatres had been used for glamour shows: women with scanty panties and so forth.

So you walk up this crowded street and everything's falling down and you can see the awning for the theatre - it's called Nasr Theatre - covered in broken neon. There's a rather shabby, mosaic entrance hall with garish colour shots of the actors in hilarious poses. And there's a hawker, describing exactly what's going on: On stage now there's a comedy with so-and-so, roll up, roll up etc. The seats are incredibly cheap, and they don't do evening performances. The first show is at 11 in the morning, and there's another one at 1 pm, one at 3 pm and then another one at 5 pm. That's because with the coming of the Revolution nightlife on Lalezar stopped dead, so the theatres just rescheduled. And at 11 o'clock in the morning the theatre is packed with every management's dream - a huge working-class male audience.

Inside there's these rather threadbare green velvet curtains and it begins with a voice-over, an intimate PA announcement telling you you're going to see this play and it's performed by this company and it features these wonderful actors. Like nineteenth-century roll-up but also like cinema credits, and you don't have to rip people off selling them programmes. First of all there's a short frontcloth scene in the manner of a prologue, where we meet the hero and his sidekick. And then the curtain judders back to some tinkly tinkly music, and you are in a world of fable, of *1001 Nights*, and there's very colourful, slightly cheap, cut-out scenery and people dressed in very gorgeous flowing robes with turbans and emeralds and sparkling accoutrements. The scenes are quite short, and then the curtains stagger back on, and there is more soothing jingly-jangly music whilst they change the scenery around behind it ready for the next stunning tableau. And the audience is absolutely rapt by it. Half way through someone came on with a microphone and sang a song for no good reason, and at the happy end the main character did a little dance, just moving his hips a fraction while the audience went wild. Then he made an announcement regarding next week's show, and as the audience left, if they really appreciated it, they'd slip the equivalent of ten pounds into his pocket.

The play I saw was being performed in rep with another company doing a different play - two shows each per day. And you could just sit there all day, they didn't clear the hall, so you could come and go as you wished, like an old-fashioned cinema, even during the show. And that's a wonderful thing, that the audience feel free to be completely engrossed by it or to get up and go to the loo. The atmosphere isn't at all hush-hush. In fact there was a fight when I went. A big squabble broke out at the back of the auditorium during the last scene. It was really very loud, and I thought: They're bound to stop now. But they didn't. They kept a close eye on what was going on, but they weren't going to stop and have to start the scene again. They weren't that precious about what they were doing, and they wanted to have their break before the next show.

The company of seven or eight actors - all traditional types: the old man, the young ingenue, the juvenile lead - had been doing it for so long they were totally bored in one sense with the whole thing but because they were so consummately professional it didn't matter at all. They were counting the house but the timing was never less than razor-sharp. What they were doing was not in any sense infected by our notions of art. This was what they did. Told the stories and made a very decent, honest crust out of it. And the theatre economy was very healthy, there was no subsidy in there, it was full and of very high quality. The leading actor, Sadi Afshar, told me afterwards that the Revolution had actually been very good for them because it had killed off all the glamour shows and placed a new emphasis on indigenous Iranian culture. Which is why Iran is probably the only 'no rap, no Coke' culture left in the world. Had the Shah remained this theatre wouldn't have been there.

I think that this type of theatre - popular but not trashy, cheap, accessible and of a quality where you want to come back week after week - is something that many of us try to create in the West. But, despite the rhetoric, it isn't possible because of the economic conditions that we live in. And more subsidy isn't the answer because that creates a whole new set of problems. This was a pure, genuine popular theatre. And I really didn't expect to see that at all. I felt: This is what I've been trying to do in the theatre in Britain for years and years and suddenly I've found it, happening naturally in a very uncontrived context.

You can go into the foyer and buy these massive slabs of ice cream sandwiched between two big wafers, as big as a loaf of bread. And people sit in the dark, watching and eating ice cream. And I remember seeing this old man's face: a huge beak nose and thousands of lines - wrinkles - all over his face and a massive mouth with no teeth, just beaming like a child at the stage, absolutely rapt. I kept staring at him. I spent more time looking at him than I did looking at the theatre. He really was completely engrossed. And that was wonderful.

CALL FOR PAPERS

Submissions are invited for Issue 4 of *Performance Practice*, a fully refereed academic journal, which offers an analytical and rigorous record of investigations into creative practical and performance work stemming from university departments world-wide. *Performance Practice* is available in standard magazine format, by subscription, or on the internet at

http://chandra.chester.ac.uk/~dmanley/perform.htm

The greater the ephemerality, the greater the need for thorough and lasting documentation; *Performance Practice* forms one aspect of the production-process, an aspect that always strives to be more provocative than prescriptive and which permits the creative event a resonance beyond its immediate, original audience.

Articles should be submitted in Word 6 HD PC disk and hard copy to the editor at the following address: John Freeman, *Performance Practice*, University College Chester, Chester CH1 4BJ, UK or e-mailed to jfreeman@chester.ac.uk

Review Board: Gerry Harris (Lancaster), Barry Edwards (Reader, Brunel), Sue Purdie (Plymouth), Marsha Meskimmon (Staffordshire), Prof. Robert Germay (Liege), Prof. James De Paul (Wisconsin), Prof. Tim Palkovic (Plattsburgh).

New Theatre Quarterly

Editors:
Clive Barker, *University of Warwick*
Simon Trussler, *University of London*

New Theatre Quarterly provides a vital international forum where theatrical scholarship and practice can meet and where prevailing dramatic assumptions can be subjected to vigorous critical questioning. It shows that theatre history has a contemporary relevance, that theatre studies need a methodology; and that theatre criticism needs a language. The journal publishes news, analysis and debate within the field of theatre studies.

Features
Articles - authoritative and often controversial
Surveys of recent developments in theatre
Reports and announcements of conferences and festivals
Book reviews of direct relevance to everybody working in the field
Contributors of the highest calibre - from critics to writers, actors to scholars

Subscription Information
Volume 13 (49-52) in 1997: February, May, August and November
£47 for institutions; £27 for individuals; prices include delivery by air.
ISSN 0266-424X

Further Information
Please send me a FREE sample copy of **New Theatre Quarterly**

Name _____

Address _____

_____

_____

_____

Return this coupon to: Journals Marketing Deparment, Cambridge Univeristy Press, *FREEPOST, The Edinburgh Building, Cambridge, CB2 1BR, UK
Tel: +44 (0)1223 325969
Fax: +44 (0)1223 315052
E-mail: journals_marketing@cup.cam.ac.uk
*No stamp necessary if posted within UK

In USA, Canada and Mexico: Cambridge University Press, 40 West 20th Street, New York, NY 1001-4211 USA
Tel: 914 937 9600 x 154 Fax: 914 937 4712
E-mail: journals_marketing@cup.org

CAMBRIDGE
UNIVERSITY PRESS

Performance Research
A Journal of Performing Arts

General Editor: **Richard Gough**
Joint Editors: **Claire MacDonald** and **Ric Allsopp**

An innovative venture, *Performance Research* is the only journal of the performing arts to speak from Europe on European work, while relating it to the wider world in geographic, critical and historical terms. The themed issues are artfully produced and fully illustrated with photographs and drawings. Volume 2 includes:

Letters from Europe
May 1997: 0-415-16178-9: £10.99
On Tourism
August 1997: 0-415-16179-7: £10.99
On Refuge
December 1997: 0-415-16180-0: £10.99

ISSN: 1352-8165
Performance Research is available in bookshops and by subscription. For subscription details, please contact **Nita Nadkarni** at our London address.

The Grotowski Sourcebook

Edited by **Richard Schechner**
and **Lisa Wolford**

The first comprehensive overview of the phases of Jerzy Grotowski's long and multi-faceted career. Featured are a unique collection of Grotowski's own writings and contributions from international theorists including Eugenio Barba, Peter Brooks, Jan Kott, Eric Bentley and Jennifer Kumiega.

Worlds of Performance

October 1997: 234x156
544pp: 34 b+w photos
Hb: 0-415-13110-3: £85.00

2nd Edition
Theatre Audiences

Susan Bennett

'**Bennett's book is enormously useful and compelling.**'
- Jill Dolan,Theatre Journal

September 1997: 216x138: 264pp
Hb: 0-415-15722-6: £40.00
Pb: 0-415-15723-4: £12.99

Routledge books are available from all good bookshops. For more information, or a **FREE** Performance Studies **catalogue**, please contact: **Cynthia Wainwright**, Routledge, 11 New Fetter Lane, London EC4P 4EE.
Tel: +44 (0)171 842 2032   Fax: +44 (0)171 842 2306
Email: info.performance@routledge.com
Routledge On-Line: http://www.routledge.com/routledge.html

ROUTLEDGE

 **SUBSCRIPTION INFORMATION**

LIVE – the polemical review of the performing arts – can be obtained through bookshops or on subscription direct from the publishers.

A new issue is published approximately every six months. Renewable subscriptions for two issues (one year) or four issues (two years) are available. A subscription is the most economic and convenient way to be sure to acquire future issues. All subscriptions include surface mail. See overleaf for subscription rates and order form.

BACK ISSUES
See overleaf for prices and order form

LIVE I
Food for the soul: a new generation of British Theatremakers
Interviews by the editor, David Tushingham, with: Bobby Baker, Matthew Bourne of Adventures in Motion Pictures, Stephen Daldry, Gloria, Paul Godfrey, Simon McBurney of Theatre de Complicite, Katie Mitchell, Lloyd Newson of DV8, Neil Wallace, Jeremy Weller of The Grassmarket Project

LIVE 2
Not what I am: the experience of performing
Interviews by the editor, David Tushingham with: Simon Russell Beale, Simon Callow, Ken Campbell, Katrin Cartlidge, Alan Mountford of Geese Theatre Co., John Hegley, Kathryn Hunter, Sue Lefton, Patrick Marber, Michael Pennington, Patsy Rodenburg, Ian Saville, Nabil Shaban, Gerald Wooster

LIVE 3
Critical Mass
A sampler of current British playwrighting, featuring extracts from plays by: Harwant Bains, Neil Bartlett, Simon Burke, Richard Cameron, Kate Dean, Helen Edmundson, David Farr, Paul Godfrey, Jonathan Harvey, Judith Johnson, Sarah Kane, Patrick Marber, Gregory Motton, Phyllis Nagy, Meredith Oakes, Joe Penhall, Philip Ridley, David Spencer, Nick Ward, Emily Woof

LIVE 4
Freedom Machine
Gives voices to artists and companies working beyond the mainstream: Beaconsfield, Blast Theory, Nigel Charnock, Tim Etchells, Ernst Fischer, John Fox, Stella Hall, Primitive Science

LIVE

ORDER FORM

Detach or photocopy this form and return it to:

Nick Hern Books
14 Larden Road
London W3 7ST
tel. +44(0) 181 740 9539
fax. +44(0) 181 746 2006

SUBSCRIPTION

I wish to subscribe to LIVE, commencing with issue no _____

(This is issue no. 5)

As an **individual** at a private address, I will pay for:

☐ 2 issues @ £12.50

☐ 4 issues @ £20.00

As an **institution** we will pay for:

☐ 2 issues @ £20.00

☐ 4 issues @ £30.00

SINGLE COPIES

☐ Please send me one copy of the next issue, LIVE 6 @ £6.99

BACK NUMBERS

Please send the back numbers of LIVE ticked below (for contents see overleaf)

☐ LIVE 1 @ £8.99

☐ LIVE 2 @ £8.99

☐ LIVE 3 @ £9.99

☐ LIVE 4 @ £7.99

[Note Live 1-3 available in limited quantity only]

All prices include surface postage.
Please add 20% for airmail

METHOD OF PAYMENT

Sender's Name _____

Address for delivery _____

_____

_____

Post/Zip code _____

Country _____

VAT registration No (EU residents only)

_____

NHB Ltd VAT no. (GB 626 1240 71)

☐ I enclose a sterling cheque/banker's draft made payable to **Nick Hern Books Ltd**

☐ Please invoice me. Purchase Order No: _____

☐ Please charge my Access/Visa account: total not to exceed the following amount _____

Card No

☐☐☐☐☐☐☐☐☐☐☐☐☐☐☐☐☐

Expiry Date

☐☐☐☐

Signature _____

Name on card and billing address (if different from above)

_____

_____

_____

Postcode _____

Please let us know if you do not want to receive any other mailings from Nick Hern Books. We do not make our mailing list available to third parties

80